New Dimensions in Foreign Policy

New Dimensions in Foreign Policy

A STUDY IN BRITISH
ADMINISTRATIVE EXPERIENCE
1947–59

MAX BELOFF

*Gladstone Professor of Government and Public
Administration in the University of Oxford*

Ruskin House
GEORGE ALLEN & UNWIN LTD
MUSEUM STREET LONDON

PRINTED IN GREAT BRITAIN
in 11 *on* 12 *point Bell type*
BY SIMSON SHAND LIMITED
LONDON, HERTFORD AND HARLOW

Preface

THE present volume seeks to contribute to the understanding of one of the most important political developments of our times, the impact upon the administration and
political systems of independent States of the network of
international organizations in whose work they are increasingly involved. For this purpose a study has been made
of one particular example; namely the effect on British
Government of Britain's adherence to the family of international organizations which came into being in the years
immediately after the Second World War in order to
meet some of the most urgent needs of Western Europe, and
which gave expression to the growing sense of community
among the western European and north-Atlantic peoples.

A large literature already exists on NATO, OEEC, the
Council of Europe and WEU, as well as on those organizations confined to the six countries of 'Little Europe', which
Britain has so far been unwilling to join. British policy in
the whole field, both economic and military, has also been
fairly exhaustively discussed. But this, I believe, is the
first attempt to see what this proliferation of organizations
has meant in terms of the actual functioning of government
in a single country. It is thus primarily, as the sub-title
indicates, a study in British administrative experience. For
it is this experience which has given meaning to the 'new
dimensions' in British foreign policy to which the title of the
book refers.

A study of contemporary administration must necessarily
be based largely upon oral evidence. For this reason my
thanks are due, in the first place, to the many individuals,
both inside and outside the public service, too numerous to
mention individually, who have freely given of their time
and trouble. I hope that this general expression of thanks
will be taken as sufficient acknowledgment. It certainly
betokens no lack of appreciation on my part.

7

I must thank the Warden and Fellows of Nuffield College for meeting out of their fund for European studies the bulk of the expenses of this enquiry, and also for providing a hospitable setting for a memorable gathering at which many of those who took part in the events described came together to discuss the lessons to be derived from them. I must also thank the Board of the Faculty of Social Studies of the University of Oxford for a grant towards my own travelling expenses.

Dr Alexander Elkin, legal adviser to the OEEC, was most generous in making it possible for me, in a short space of time, to meet a large number of persons connected with international organizations having their headquarters in Paris.

I am much indebted to Mrs R. H. Ullman (*née* Crosfield) who was my research assistant during the major part of the enquiry, and to my own secretary, Mrs P. Utechin, for valuable help throughout. Professor F. M. G. Willson, then fellow of Nuffield College, read the whole study in draft and made most valuable suggestions, as did Mr Uwe Kitzinger at the proof stage.

It is clear that the ultimate utility of studies of this kind depends a great deal upon the availability of comparative material from other countries. I anticipate that this book will be only the first in a series of treatments of one of the major problems of modern government, to culminate in a more general study which I hope one day to be in a position to write.

In as far as the present volume is concerned, I must make it clear that all the views expressed are my own, and have no official sanction of any kind. For any errors of fact that may have crept into my narrative I must also take full responsibility.

MAX BELOFF

All Souls College
Oxford
September 1960

8

Contents

———————

Contents

CHAPTER 1

The Setting

THE history of government deals with the adaptation of institutions to the constant succession of new problems, which those engaged in operating them have to face, in the light of their traditional intellectual habits and methods of work. The governments of all the principal countries of the western world have been confronted, since the end of the Second World War, with the results of a radical change in the conditions of international life. The recognition of their interdependence for welfare and defence has been a thing of uneven growth, partly because of the fluctuations in the apparent intensity of the threat from the alternative system of world communism, and partly because of the popular desire to transcend the threat itself and to establish the interdependence of nations on a world basis.

Much international activity has been devoted to the construction of international institutions designed to facilitate the working together of like-minded countries in the political, military and economic fields. The unfinished story of these developments, particularly in relation to Western Europe and North America, has been extensively studied and the many alternative designs for the future thoroughly canvassed.[1]

For the historian of government, however, there is an equally important aspect of these developments that has so far received very much less attention. It remains a fact that the principal burden in the promotion and execution of policies falls ultimately upon the governments of the separate nations, and that the work of the international organizations themselves is, at present, principally, though no longer exclusively, a reflection of this

---

[1] See, for instance, the PEP Study *European Organizations* (London: Allen & Unwin, 1959) and A. H. Robertson, *European Institutions: Co-operation, Integration, Unification* (London, 1959).

activity. In order, therefore, the better to understand the international scene, it is necessary to examine the extent to which the different governments have proved themselves competent in this sphere; whether we estimate competence by their ability to secure the best results from the point of view of the peoples to whom they are severally responsible; or whether we take the standpoint of the interests of the international community as a whole.

It is obvious that a definitive study along these lines will have to await the opening of the archives to the future historian. Few, if any, governments reveal sufficient of their international policies for contemporary assessment of success and failure to be anything more than provisional. On the other hand, it is possible to trace, at least in part, the impact of these developments and policies upon the actual structure of government, and provisionally to assess the extent to which the traditional relationships between legislatures, ministers and civil servants have been, or are being, affected by the new demands made upon them—remembering always how difficult it is to disentangle those which proceed directly from the demands of the new international environment from those which are simply the result of the contemporary accretions to the powers of government taken as a whole.[1]

Studies of this kind should, therefore, ideally fufil a dual purpose. They should enable one to obtain a more realistic understanding of the way in which international society actually functions, and they should also help one to understand certain fundamental characteristics of the different governmental structures by seeing how they behave when confronted with roughly similar problems. It is clear that only the examination of a number of separate governments will provide adequate answers, even within this limited field. The present study, which is limited to the government of the United Kingdom, is therefore intended only as a contribution to this wider enquiry.[2]

[1] On this point see my inaugural lecture *The Tasks of Government* (Oxford University Press, 1958).

[2] On October 21, 1959, the North Atlantic Council accepted a recommendation from the North Atlantic Studies Committee to the effect that a series of studies of this kind would be highly desirable, and that the North Atlantic Studies Committee should try to arrange for enquiries to be set on foot in a number of member countries of NATO. It is hoped that this initiative will produce a number of studies for different countries following substantially the pattern of the present volume.

Even if the scope of the investigation is limited in this way it raises a number of questions of method and presentation. While it is necessary to avoid telling over again the familiar story of the response of the Western European countries and North-America to the economic and military dangers of the post-war period, some account of this response is required if the particular character of the British contribution to it is to be fully comprehensible. Furthermore, the impact upon the British governmental structure was not an immediate one, nor the result of a conscious thought-out long-term plan; the relevant British machinery developed alongside the international institutions to which it corresponded, and was continually modified so as to meet their changing demands. Again, while this development in time must be followed, it is as important to see the particular devices of government we are concerned with in their relation to the general governmental and political system of which they form only part.

The present work, then, falls roughly into two parts. In the first four chapters the subject matter is handled episodically, the developments at home being treated in relation to the swiftly changing scene abroad. In the last four chapters a synoptic view is taken, the British system being now looked at as a whole in the light of certain general questions, all raised, in their different ways, by the succession of events described in the earlier part of the book.

A treatment of this kind inevitably involves a certain amount of overlapping and even of repetition, but this has seemed a relatively small price to pay in order to avoid the distortion which either a straightforward narrative or a purely analytical approach would entail. It means also that, in the early chapters in particular, some fairly rapid changes of scale are unavoidable. One has to pass from major issues of international politics and organization, to what might appear to be minor questions of domestic convenience. But one may hazard a guess that in so doing we are closer to reproducing the real world of politics than is sometimes the case in those more formal treatises that find room only for great men making great decisions. Some history is like that but much of it, and much administrative history in particular, is concerned with the outcome of a multitude of unspectacular decisions arrived at in response to the relentless flood of paper that crosses the desk of the busy minister or civil servant between the in-tray and the out.

The British case offers both advantages and disadvantages to the student of these problems. On the one hand, the British system of government, although considerably affected by the experience of the Second World War, preserved an unbroken continuity, differing in this way from many of its European neighbours. Because of this, it is easier to isolate the impact upon its traditional organization of successive new demands. Furthermore, it is a system in which the various parts are highly conscious of their own status and functions, and in which any changes are likely to be examined fairly closely in the light of an accepted body of doctrine. Again, British experience differs from the American experience in that the principal official positions concerned with the making and execution of policy are held by career civil servants, unaffected by changes in the political complexion of successive administrations.

We can therefore assume a degree of continuity in personnel at the highest levels, which should make it easier to distinguish between general changes of attitude and the impact of particular individual opinions. Although there was a change of government in 1951 at an important juncture in the story we shall be trying to follow, the issues we are concerned with appear to have been mainly thought of in non-party terms, so that without minimizing the opinions of individual ministers, it is possible to regard the political figures in the story as also forming part of a single and fairly homogeneous group dominating the two front benches of the House of Commons throughout the period.

The disadvantages of using Britain as an example arise from the particularly complex set of international relationships in which Britain is necessarily involved as a result of her peculiar position in the world. While Britain, in common with the other major states of western and central Europe, has suffered an undoubted recession in her standing as a Power, in consequence of the changing scale according to which national strength is calculated, and has clearly had to accommodate herself to Middle Power rather than Great Power status, the implications of this for policy have been much less easy to assess than has been the case with regard to some other countries. In other words, because of the dominant importance of overseas commerce in her economy, her peculiar ties with the independent members of the Commonwealth, her responsibilities for the remaining dependencies and her aspirations to a special relationship with the United States, Britain has been unable to accept a limitation of her interests to a single continent, Europe. She remained, after the Second World War, a Power with world-wide interests and responsibilities, though no longer in the strict sense a World Power.

To work out the positive consequences that should follow from these generally accepted facts, was, perhaps, the single most important task that confronted Britain's rulers, whether in Westminster or in Whitehall. It was partially obscured, particularly perhaps in the early part of this period, by the simultaneous emergence of major items of controversy in domestic politics and by the rapidity of social changes and institutional development at home. But in the minds of those responsible for Britain's destinies, if not so obviously in the instincts of the electorate, the development of the welfare state at home was in fact going to be conditioned by the extent to which the correct solution could be found to the external problems of British policy.

It could, indeed, be argued that because of this very concentration of the electorate upon Britain's domestic concerns, the policy makers had an unusually free hand to experiment in the external field where public opinion was only likely to be roused if confronted with the major issues of war and peace. The general tone of relations between the West and the Soviet Union was a matter of constant concern, but the precise nature of the relations between Britain and the other countries of the free world was largely left to be decided by specialists. It is partly because of this fact, indeed, that one is justified in trying to isolate the structural and administrative aspects of these problems from policy as the economist and strategist would define it.

It was common ground among those concerned with these matters, that there was no possibility of Britain conducting her own policies under any form of isolation, in that she did not now possess the resources which could make such a wholly independent policy possible. By taking part in the foundation of the United Nations Organization and by active participation in its work and in that of other international institutions aiming at universal membership. Britain renewed its pre-war commitment to the idea of securing the widest possible participation of the countries of the world in the tasks of maintaining the peace and promoting the general welfare. Since, however, it was clear from the beginning, and even more patently so in 1947, that there were serious limits to the extent to which universalist institutions could operate in a world deeply divided by the clash of ideologies, it was understandable that Britain should concern herself most with those countries or groupings of countries towards which she stood in a special relationship.

It was at this point that the complexities of Britain's position began to make themselves felt since, as we have seen, it was not immediately obvious with which grouping of countries Britain should regard her future as most intimately linked, or indeed whether it was necessary to make a choice between the respective demands made by the alternative ideals of a Commonwealth, a European, or an Atlantic, that is Anglo-American, future.

In 1947 no serious person could deny the importance of any one of these three principal aspects of Britain's relations. It is equally clear, however, that the correct order of priorities was differently assessed by different people. These differences may have arisen in part from the different kinds of experience that persons in public life or in the administration had had in the past, or alternatively, from circumstances directly connected with the kind of problems with which they were now directly concerned. All the active participants in these affairs seem to have had in common a repudiation of any strong ideological preference for one direction of advance as against another. There seems to have been no reflection in government circles of the idea, still sometimes echoed in the press, according to which British policy could afford to concern itself wholly with the development of closer links with the Commonwealth countries and the further progress of the dependent Empire. There was no revival of the fifty-year old notion of imperial federation as a solution to Britain's problems in the second half of the twentieth century. While it would be untrue to say that no enthusiasts for the idea of a united Europe ever found their way into the political and official world in Britain, the concept of Britain merging its identity into some form of European union, as a desirable objective in itself, was not seriously entertained in any influential quarter. Indeed, it must be admitted that there was some failure to appreciate the strength of sentiments of this kind among the nationals of certain continental countries.

This failure, which might perhaps be described as a failure of the imagination, may have been due to the very continuity of Britain's own institutional experience already referred to. It was perhaps insufficiently clear to any but a small minority in Britain that the countries of continental Europe had received such a major shock, as a result of their wartime and immediately post-war experiences, that they were ready to experiment with quite new forms of international organization, even where these appeared to involve a substantial departure from the traditional autonomy of the nation state. With, in some cases, fewer of the inhibitions arising from Britain's complex overseas relationships, it was more possible on the continent to take a fairly straight-forward view of the implications of the new situation. If their economies were individually too small to take full advantage of modern technology, then let them be pooled. If their military forces could not in themselves guarantee national defence, then let them be merged into some wider unity; and if these changes called for different political institutions, these were not excluded either.

This is not to say that views of this kind were held by a majority of the people or even of the leaders in any single European country. It is only to say that the problems could be discussed in terms which went beyond the range of British thinking, which itself continued to take for granted the existence and traditional responsibilities of the nation's own political system.

The most positive enthusiasm in governmental circles in Britain was that for a continuance or renewal of the Anglo-American Alliance. No Foreign Secretary in the period ever lost sight of the fact that the defence of Europe, and hence of Britain, was inconceivable without American participation, and that it must be a fundamental objective of British policy to see that this was always forthcoming. Upon this point there could be agreement indeed between Britain and some of the would-be architects of a European federation, although the latter visualized a close European union without Britain as a major independent partner in some future Atlantic alliance or community.

There was indeed to be a further complication in that the United States, while generally favourable to the idea of some form of European integration as a barrier to communist expansion, was inclined in this respect to treat Britain for these purposes as part of Europe rather than as the separate entity which it represented in the minds of British policy makers. Taken together with the American insistence on the principle of commercial non-discrimination, this was to provide an element of ambiguity in the Anglo-American relationship never fully to be resolved in our period.

A number of obstacles confronted those policy makers who were in 1947 particularly concerned with fostering the continuation of the Anglo-American alliance. The breakdown of the Anglo-American drive for a single world economy based upon the principle of the widest possible multilateralism had revealed and for a time aggravated certain basic differences of outlook. As the historian of this phase in the economic history of Anglo-American relations has written: 'The United States pressed for non-discrimination both in and out of season and adopted an unbecoming evangelism in its assault on the sterling area and Imperial Preference. British opinion, in turn, yielded to an overweening insistence on the sanctity of these institutions and of ambitious programmes of domestic expansion. The resulting controversies inflamed public opinion and impeded essential adjustments in national policy. They led eventually to immoderate and inflexible positions not founded in the genuine interests of the two countries.'[1]

A less immediate impact on public opinion was produced by the unilateral abrogation by the Americans of the wartime cooperation in the development of atomic energy for military purposes.[2] Since the general public in Britain was naturally most concerned with the redeployment of the national resources for peaceful reconstruction, military considerations were once again remote. Nevertheless, the fact that the two countries were now independently pursuing research and development in what was recognized to be the decisive weapon in any future conflict, for-

---

[1] R. N. Gardner, *Sterling-Dollar Diplomacy* (Oxford University Press, 1956), p. 384.

[2] The MacMahon Act which prevented further co-operation in the atomic field was signed by President Truman on August 1, 1946. For his correspondence with the British Government on this topic see *The Memoirs of H. S. Truman* (New York and London, 1956), Vol. II, Ch. I. Co-operation was renewed after the Amendment to the MacMahon Act signed by President Eisenhower on July 2, 1958.

bade that close intimacy in strategic planning which had been a feature of the wartime partnership, and which formally came to an end with the dissolution of the formal machinery for co-operation between the two sets of Chiefs of Staff.[1]

In the eyes of British people, the American military were now so confident of their country's independent power that they could afford to isolate themselves and their thinking from their former and prospective allies. On the other hand, the State Department, like the Foreign Office, remained conscious of the many areas in which an alignment between British and American policy was, or might prove to be, desirable so that the slackening of ties on the military side had no political parallel. Even on the military side, important contacts were maintained, and no doubt the personal friendships of wartime accounted for something here also. How important these contacts remained is again something upon which only the future historian will be able to pronounce; for after the establishment of more general ties through the North Atlantic Treaty Organization, it became politically desirable to minimize the extent of private Anglo-American contacts in order not to upset the susceptibilities of other partners in the new alliance. It was not only in military matters that this previous experience of Anglo-American co-operation was to prove important. Some of the key figures in Whitehall, who made themselves spokesmen for the view that the Anglo-American connection should be given an absolute priority, had taken an important part on the civilian side of the joint war effort of the two countries.

A further point made by the protagonists of the American alliance, was that any form that it might take would be easier to fit in with Britain's Commonwealth obligations than the kind of demands which were being voiced by the Europeans. American hostility to the idea of empire and, on another plane, preferential economic arrangements between Britain and other Commonwealth countries had not adversely affected its appeal in this res-

[1] Originally it was agreed to keep the Combined Chiefs of Staff Committee in existence until the signature of the Peace Treaties. It was not then realized how far off an event this was likely to be. In fact, the machinery was allowed to run down and rapidly lost its wartime importance, particularly in view of the recovery by the State Department of the major responsibility for the conduct of foreign policy. The final demise of the Committee was announced on September 28, 1949, by which time, of course, new channels of consultation in connection with the North Atlantic Treaty had already been opened up. See W. H. McNeill, *America, Britain and Russia, their Co-operation and Conflict* (London, Oxford University Press, 1953), p. 679.

pect. Some of the older Commonwealth countries were now convinced that they had to look to the United States rather than to Britain for military assistance, while the newer members of the Commonwealth recognized in the United States the main available source of the capital they so urgently required for their own development.

In very general terms it could be said that by 1959 the order of priorities held by most influential people in Whitehall had not seriously changed from what it had been in 1947. The critics of Britain's handling of these problems were therefore to be found mainly among those who believe that there were positive advantages to be gained for Britain in adopting the role of a leading partner in the movement for a United Europe.

Criticism of this kind is based upon several different lines of argument. There are those who believe that the idea of recovering a special relationship to the United States, analogous to the wartime one, was based upon a fundamental misunderstanding of America's own attitudes, and that Britain would be in a stronger position within the Atlantic Alliance if she could speak in unison with her European neighbours. America, it is held, was less directly interested than the British have tended to assume in the maintenance of Britain's world position, and always felt able to deal directly with Commonwealth countries where her own interests were concerned. On the other hand, the importance of Western Europe, which has made very rapid economic progress during these years under consideration, has much increased. A proper relationship with the European economy is thus a vital British interest. These considerations are fortified by the view that Britain misunderstood the state of affairs in Western Europe in the immediately post-war years, when there was a general turning away from the idea of the self-sufficiency of the national state, and that a positive lead by Britain in that period would have been widely welcomed on the continent. As a result of our failure to accept this role we have come it is felt, to be regarded, as a major obstacle to constructive effort in Europe and this has resulted in turn in our growing unpopularity and in our possible exclusion from markets and opportunities vital to us. Although, as we have seen, the British were on the whole unconvinced by protestations of a desire for greater unity on the part of the continental Europeans in the early years of this period, by the end of 1959 it was more difficult to dismiss the reality of the drive towards European integration. It is possible, therefore, that this study is being written at a time when the general framework of ideas about British policy is being subjected to serious reconsideration for the first time since 1947.

But in the period with which we are concerned it was fairly consistently argued that Britain could not enter into arrangements by which aspects of her own government's responsibility would be transferred to international authorities not answerable to the British parliament, and so ultimately to the British electorate. It was generally held that the only alternative to maintaining British sovereignty in this sense was to enter into some form of federal arrangement, and it was believed, as a result of experience with federal institutions, particularly in the Commonwealth, that in any modern federal system, the governments of the units would have to take a wholly subordinate place. This argument, particularly when used as an obstacle to Britain's entering into certain European institutions, was often fortified by the consideration that a diminution of British sovereignty would make impossible the methods of free consultation between uncommitted partners through which the Commonwealth operates. This was however, generally speaking, secondary to the question of the prerogatives of parliament at home.

The British were prepared to make, and did upon occasion make, what appeared to be surrenders of their freedom of action in specific fields but these were thought of as analogous to provisions in conventional treaties of alliance, and not as derogating in any permanent respect from the authority of the British Government. Apart from these specific concessions, there was a marked British preference for institutions whose *raison d'être* was the improvement of the facilities for consultation between independent and sovereign governments. It was generally agreed that there were many fields in which the harmonization of British policy with that of a group of associated countries was desirable or even essential, but it was believed as firmly, that this harmonization could be achieved by the methods of consultation and negotiation, and that the execution of the policies arrived at could normally be entrusted to the individual governments exercising the authority conferred upon them by their own constitutional systems.

21

While this general line of argument remained fairly constant throughout the period from 1947 to 1959 in regard to economic matters, there is some evidence that technological changes in the sphere of weapons were giving it less plausibility as far as matters of defence were concerned. By 1959 it was possible for persons who had been closely concerned with the military aspects of the Atlantic Alliance to assert that it could not, under present day conditions, fulfil the tasks allotted to it without a substantial delegation of certain activities and of rights of decision in an emergency to some central authority.[1]

This institutional conservatism, where relations with the external world were concerned, merely reflected the fact that the British at home were, to some degree, unconscious of the extent to which the domestic continuity to which we have referred, merely obscured what were actually profound changes in emphasis within the governmental structure. Politics, at any rate at home, could still be thought of and discussed in terms of the clash of rival political parties and the impact of powerful ministers. The formidable galaxy of talent in the Labour Government of 1945 and its rapid passage of an important programme of reforming legislation revived memories of 1868 and 1905; no less formidable was the seasoned team which Sir Winston Churchill led back into the seats of power in 1951, and which, under different leadership, was still in command at the end of our period. The fact that in the rather specialized field with which we are concerned, the accent must often seem to be on the administrator rather than on the statesman, must not lead us to forget that ultimately foreign policy, like domestic policy, was determined through the operation of the democratic process, in which the symbol in Britain is the Cabinet of responsible ministers, at once party leaders and executants of national policies.[2]

The war years themselves had seen a number of innovations in British Government, some temporary, others of a more permanent kind. Their tendency was inevitably a centralizing one. The Cabinet Office had been used to an increasing extent as an instrument of co-ordination, and certain central services had been at-

[1] Alastair Buchan, *NATO in the 1960s*; a report of the Institute of Strategic Studies (London, 1960).

[2] cf. Max Beloff, *Foreign Policy and the Democratic Process* (Baltimore: London, 1955).

tached to it—an Economic Section and a Central Statistical Office. On the other hand, while the Minister of Defence existed in the person of the Prime Minister, the Ministry of Defence did not come into being as a separate department until December 1946.[1]

Nevertheless, in many respects, the administrative questions that would require solution in the post-war years could be identified by direct reference to experience before 1939. Already, at that time, the traditional divisions of the subject matter of government were beginning to wear thin.

The principal problem of co-ordination in the inter-war years had been that created by the increasing role of economic questions in the formulation and conduct of foreign policy. In departmental terms this was a question of the right relationship between the Foreign Office itself, the Treasury and the Board of Trade. The handling of commercial matters had been settled by the creation in 1917 of an independent department, the Department of Overseas Trade. The abolition of this department in 1946, when its work devolved upon the Board of Trade, was an indication that the reshaping of the Foreign Office for its new and enlarged responsibilities was making satisfactory progress.

The most significant outward manifestation of this new conception of the duties of the Foreign Office had been the merging, in 1943, of the Foreign Office, the Diplomatic Service, the Consular Service, the Commercial Diplomatic Service and certain sections of the information services into a single foreign service.[2]

More difficult might appear to have been the question of the future relations of the Foreign Office with the Treasury. It was held by a number of people, that some of the now admitted weaknesses of British foreign policy in the inter-war years had been due to the encroachment by the Treasury upon the rights and prerogatives of the Foreign Office. They had in mind the claims allegedly made by Sir Warren Fisher in his capacity as Head of the Civil Service to have a say in the making of the principal diplomatic appointments, and to control the distribution of papers to

[1] For changes in the structure of British Government in the period see D. N. Chester and F. M. G. Willson, *The Organization of British Central Government 1914 to 1956* (London: Allen & Unwin, 1957).

[2] See the White Paper, *Proposals for the Reform of the Foreign Service* (Cmd. 6420, 1943), printed as an appendix to *The Foreign Office*, by Lord Strang (London: Allen & Unwin, 1955).

the Cabinet. In their view the essential thing was that the whole range of foreign affairs should come within the scope of the Foreign Office, and that the responsibility of the foreign secretary should be undiluted.[1] It has been suggested, however, on good authority, that these critics confused two separate issues, the administrative interventions of the Treasury and the view held by the Treasury that economic affairs were its concern alone and that the Foreign Office should be confined to the more traditional spheres of diplomacy.[2]

Whatever the truth of these matters—and the critics are not always in accord about their criticisms—it is clear that the belief that our pre-war errors of policy had to some extent represented a failure in co-ordination, was very much alive in the minds of those responsible for shaping the machinery of government in the post-war world.

The formal independence of the Foreign Office was recognized in the reforms of 1943, when the new combined foreign service was separated from the home civil service; and on October 1, 1956, when the Secretary of the Cabinet was also appointed to be Joint Permanent Secretary to the Treasury, he was given the designation of Head of the Home Civil Service. But these changes did not mean in any sense a separation of the work of the Foreign Office from that of government as a whole. Side by side with the growth of the economic work of the Foreign Office itself, new machinery for interdepartmental co-operation was created, and new informal relationships were established with other departments in order to facilitate the closest co-operation in day-to-day work. By the end of the period, it was possible to claim that, at any rate in the economic field, British foreign policy could be looked at as an operation carried out by government as a whole, with no single department claiming priority. It was held that the problems of interdepartmental rivalry, noted in earlier periods in Britain and still extant in other countries, had largely disappeared. Where there appeared to be important differences it was urged that these might well come from political considerations of which the Ministers themselves were principally conscious rather than from the particular attitudes of the several departments.

[1] See Sir Walford Selby, *Diplomatic Twilight* 1930–40 (London, 1953); Sir Victor Wellesley, *Diplomacy in Fetters* (London, 1954).
[2] See Lord Percy of Newcastle, *Some Memories* (London, 1958).

It is important, as we have said, to emphasize the role of the Ministers at the head of the different departments which were, together, responsible for the making and execution of foreign policy in the area in which this study is concerned. The classical view of the British system, that it was for ministers to determine policy and for civil servants merely to place them in a position in which they could take the correct decisions, was firmly adhered to in Whitehall. There were those outside government who believed that under modern conditions this abstract constitutional position bore less and less relation to the facts, and that the modern civil servant must accept the fact that the increasing complexity and technicality of Government made it inevitable that he should play a real part in policy formation. But the contrary view held the field, at least as far as public statements by persons with official experience was concerned.[1]

In any event, the constitutional responsibility of ministers was insisted upon both by their civil servants and by Parliament itself—Parliamentary interest in such a subject as the new international institutions might be intermittent and lukewarm, but the possibility of an account being demanded could never be ignored. There were thus good reasons for adhering to the position that the co-ordination of policy was primarily a matter for ministers, and must be settled either in cabinet committees or in the last resort in the Cabinet itself, where the influence of the Prime Minister might well be decisive.

It was this feeling, that decision-making must be concentrated in the Cabinet itself, that was no doubt in part responsible for the fact that the machinery of the old Committee of Imperial Defence was not revived after the end of the war.[2] It was suggested by Lord Hankey who had had much to do with the elaboration of this machinery that it had the great advantage of permitting the association with the Government of the day, when desirable, of Opposition representatives, and so far as they wished it, of representatives of the independent members of the Commonwealth. His idea was that there might now be a standing sub-committee of the CID on Foreign Affairs, served by sub-committees of officials, including one which should specifically be charged with

---

[1] See e.g. C. H. Sisson, *The Spirit of British Administration* (London, 1959).

[2] On its history before the Second World War, see John Ehrman, *Cabinet Government and War* (Cambridge, 1958).

co-ordinating the work of the Foreign Office, which was to have the leading role with that of the economic departments.[1]

Instead of this, there were to be in the post-war period the Cabinet itself, its own committees and associated committees of officials, treated as cabinet committees in so far as they were serviced by the now enlarged cabinet secretariat.[2] The relations between such official committees, essential if the work was to be digested into manageable form, and the ministerial committees, raised important administrative and indeed constitutional difficulties.

When, as in the case of the immediately post-war government, a fairly consistent attempt was made to have official committees serving ministerial committees with the same scope and terms of reference, it was possible for ministers to argue when a matter came before them, that their point of view had already been accepted at the official level and that there was therefore no room for further discussion. Ministers naturally dislike a situation in which they appear to be confronted with a *fait accompli*, particularly since they have the constitutional responsibility for a collective decision and this cannot be devolved upon officials.

For this reason the new government formed in 1951 by Mr Churchill (as he then was), did away with the existing structure of official committees and began with purely ministerial control of business. It proved impossible, however, not to devolve business upon officials, and a compromise was reached later on whereby there was in some fields, e.g. civil defence, a close parallelism between the ministerial and the official committees, while in others no such parallelism existed. For instance, no official committee was set up corresponding to the ministerial committee dealing with home affairs, and no ministerial committee corresponding to the official committee which was established to handle NATO business. If the latter required collective ministerial approval for something, it had to go to the Defence Committee of the Cabinet, which had, of course, much wider terms of reference.

On the economic side, a ministerial committee now covered a

[1] See his lecture, 'The Control of External Affairs' given at Chatham House on October 11, 1945 and reprinted in his *Diplomacy by Conference* (London, 1946).

[2] There is a brief description of the current status of the system of cabinet committees in Sir Ivor Jennings' *Cabinet Government* (3rd ed. Cambridge, 1959), pp. 255-61.

whole range of domestic and overseas questions, which were sub-divided between different official committees. For collective min-isterial decisions these had to refer back to the main ministerial committee.

From the point of view of nomenclature, a Cabinet Committee is defined not by membership, but by whether or not it is serviced by the Cabinet Office. The Cabinet Office provides the secretariat for committees, either because they are concerned with so many different departments, or because they are closely linked to the work of a ministerial committee, or because they are so closely concerned with a policy of major interest to Ministers that they qualify as Cabinet Committees. On the other hand, the Cabinet Office resists demands to provide a secretariat for matters which, while concerning more than one department, are the primary affair of a particular department. For instance, the Cabinet Office at one time provided the secretariat for a committee on tariffs, but it was later agreed that the Board of Trade should run this for itself. Similarly, when the Ministry of Defence was formed, it took over a number of committees of officials which, during and immediately after the war, had been looked after by the Cabinet Office. The latter, of course, continues to take care of all minis-terial committees and the Secretary to the Cabinet, as the Prime Minister's principal official adviser, is the person immediately responsible for seeing to the creation of any new machinery that circumstances may call for.

These general principles of governmental organization in Britain, may have been reinforced in people's minds by wartime experiences which bore some analogy to the kind of problems created for Whitehall by the economic crisis of 1947–8, and the defence problems of 1948–50. For instance, there was the network of committees set up on an Anglo-French basis in December 1939, which was given a secretariat by the Cabinet Office with two members of the Foreign Office seconded to it as its nucleus.[1]

This rather elaborate organization naturally came to an end with the fall of France in the following summer, and the problem of Lend-Lease required a new organization to enable the White-hall departments to handle relations with other American

[1] See W. K. Hancock and M. M. Gowing, *British War Economy* (London, 1949), pp. 186 ff.

suppliers and the many problems of unfamiliar methods and terminology involved.

Although actual communications with Americans were routed through the Foreign Office, their substance was clearly not a Foreign Office matter. The general problem was handled at first by a special American section in the Cabinet Office. Later, as the separate departments became familiar with the new techniques required of them, the importance of this special section declined. Instead a vast network of joint Anglo-American agencies was set up to handle the supply problems of the forces and the allocation of scarce resources.[1]

It has further been pointed out that under war conditions formal committee work was of relatively secondary importance. The principal British civil servants were working in close proximity with each other and were constantly in touch so as to adapt their activities to the rapidly changing demands of the situation. It has been said that 'formal committee decisions were perhaps among the least important of the devices of the central machine save on purely statistical matters'.[2] Much more important was seeing that the people at the top knew exactly at any time what was going on.

It was within this general development of the techniques of British Government that the particular problems posed by the creation of the new international institutions were met and solved. Each initiative, whether British in origin or suggested by by some foreign government, demanded action in three successive stages. In the first place, the decision had to be taken as to whether to reject or to accept the suggestion in principle. If the answer was favourable, the form of the new institution had to be considered and worked out in the course of negotiations with Britain's prospective partners. This was the case with OEEC, The Council of Europe, NATO, WEU and the Free Trade Association of the 'Seven'. If it was rejected at the outset as in the case of the Schuman Plan for the European Coal and Steel Community, a watching brief had to be maintained, and proposals developed for the degree of British association with the new body that was found to be necessary. Finally, there was the more complicated case of the Common Market and Euratom, where Britain parti-

[1] See H. Duncan Hall, *North American Supply* (London, 1955).
[2] D. N. Chester ed. *Lessons of the British War Economy* (Cambridge, 1951), p. 21.

cipated in the preliminary technical discussions but was asked to withdraw at the point at which binding decisions had to be made. There followed the long and abortive negotiations for a Free Trade Area which repeated over a wider field and on a much more ambitious scale negotiations for external association that had followed the setting up of the ECSC.

In every case, where a new organization was set up, there was the problem of arranging for British representation to it and its control—and in relation to those organizations—the majority—of which Britain was itself a member, there was also the question of seeing that such decisions of the organization as were binding upon her were carried into effect. In the case of the Council of Europe this stage was preceded by decisions as to the signature and ratification of conventions negotiated under its auspices.

Finally, in order to keep in mind a complete picture of the framework of Britain's external relations in our period, it is essential to remember that Britain was a founder member of the United Nations Organization and collaborated actively in all the various institutions set up under its aegis.[1] It will not, however, be necessary, except on certain topics, to deal with this aspect of affairs in the present study, since it rapidly became clear that the United Nations and its associated bodies represented little more than a bringing up to date of the work performed by the League of Nations in the inter-war years.[2] Such work was mainly of a diplomatic nature and did not therefore present new problems from either a constitutional or an administrative point of view.

With regard to the United Nations itself, it should, however, be noted that a more substantial permanent delegation was required than had been the case with the League of Nations, owing to the greater complexity of the organization and to the provisions for more frequent meetings of its constituent organs. The fact that the headquarters of the United Nations was situated on the other side of the Atlantic was also of some importance in this

[1] The work by G. L. Goodwin, *Britain and the United Nations* (London, 1957), gives a full account of the main policies adopted by the UK on matters which came before the UN in its first decade, but unfortunately leaves outside its scope any consideration of the machinery through which its policy was formulated and presented.

[2] For a general assessment of the United Nations in our period, see H. G. Nicholas, *The United Nations as a Political Institution* (London, 1959).

connection, although the travelling time between London and New York was rapidly reduced to less than the ordinary land and sea journey to Geneva in the pre-war period. The activities of the delegation were also affected in one very important respect by the decision to have the organization situated in the United States, namely its consequent exposure to the mass media of publicity and in particular to television. This exposure involved demanding from our permanent representatives at the United Nations a capacity for using these instruments to the best advantage.

Of more relevance to our own subject have been the activities of certain other bodies organized on a worldwide basis, because they directly impinged upon British policy within the regional organizations with which we shall be concerned. British officials concerned with economic and financial policy in the widest sense were particularly anxious not to detract from the authority and influence of the wider bodies. The most important of these commitments has probably been British membership of GATT, the General Agreement on Tariffs and Trade, signed at Geneva in 1947. Despite the acceptance in principle in 1948 and 1954 by the participating countries of the desirability of creating an International Trade Organization, this has not come into being; GATT itself has functioned through periodic conferences mainly concerned with the reduction of tariffs. From the point of view of the actions incumbent upon governments in relation to GATT, it is worth noting that ordinary decisions can be taken by voting, the countries having a single vote each, with a two-thirds majority required for a waiver of obligations undertaken and for the admission of new members.

The other important organizations under this head are the International Monetary Fund and the International Bank for Reconstruction and Development, set up under the Bretton Woods agreements of 1944. These organizations are both primarily intergovernmental. In the case of the International Bank for Reconstruction and Development, decisions of the Board of Directors are taken by weighted voting according to the size of a particular country's contribution to the capital fund. Here, however, recent developments, which have fixed attention on its possible role in assisting under-developed countries, have tended to enhance the personal authority of its President and to give its permanent staff a certain independent status in world economic affairs.

Nevertheless, even these important institutions have not required any major modification in the way in which British policy is handled, though their existence, together with that of the United Nations itself and its ancillary bodies, focused attention at an early stage upon the need for some machinery for co-ordinating the policies put forward by British representatives at their respective meetings. By 1950 a fairly elaborate organization had come into existence for this purpose.[1]

At the centre there was a Steering Committee on International Organizations created in May 1946. The chairman of this committee was a senior Foreign Office official; its other members were senior officials in the other ministries concerned. The committee was served by a secretariat jointly staffed by the Foreign Office and the Cabinet Office, and its papers and minutes were circulated to most ministries. A good deal of the work was delegated to sub-committees or working parties consisting of representatives of the Ministries primarily interested, and these reported from time to time to the Steering Committee. By 1950, there were working parties on the following topics: Social Affairs, Freedom of Information, the Work of the Economic Commissions, Human Rights, Administrative and Budgetary Questions, Population and Vital Statistics, and the Status of Women. These bodies were normally active only when their subject matter was about to come before or was actually before, one or other organ of the United Nations.

Early in 1946, a Trade Negotiations Committee was set up, with the Board of Trade supplying the Chairman, and this dealt with the preliminary work on the trade negotiations leading up to the abortive charter of the proposed International Trade Organization and to GATT. These negotiations were primarily the responsibility of the Board of Trade, but the Committee enable other Ministries to bring their voice to bear on particular matters. In general the Committee worked through small working groups or sub-committees.

A committee to deal with the work of FAO was set up with a chairman from the Ministry of Food. In March 1946, an inter-

[1] See *United Kingdom Administration and International Organizations* (Royal Institute of Public Administration, February 1951).

departmental panel on international health was sponsored by the Ministry of Health to prepare briefs for the British delegation to WHO. Finally, in 1948, a Committee on Overseas Scientific Relations was set up including representatives of universities and other national bodies concerned with scientific research.

It is clear that the Steering Committee was not intended itself to have any policy making functions, and that it was primarily a clearing house for information about the work of the special committees necessitated by Britain's membership of the specialized international organizations within the United Nations family. It has been useful in enabling a number of questions to be disposed of at official level which might otherwise have had to be dealt with by the Cabinet, but a great deal of the work is remote from the major preoccupations of British policy makers.

On one point however, a United Nations agency does come directly within the orbit of this enquiry. This is the Economic Commission for Europe, set up by the Economic and Social Council of the United Nations in March 1947, which met for the first time in May of that year.[1] The ECE works primarily through specialized committees, though these do not normally meet very often. But its practical contributions to European economic life have been very small, owing to the lack of basic political agreement between its communist and non-communist members, which has led to its utilization largely as a forum for propaganda. It has, however, been argued that some of the committees have done good work, especially at times of shortage, for instance the Coal Committee, and that there are occasional technical matters upon which co-operation is possible despite the ideological divide. Many of the committees of course, deal with the same questions though in a wider geographical setting as the committees subsequently set up by OEEC.

British Government departments which have to find representatives for these committees are naturally concerned to avoid duplication. The Ministry of Power, for instance, has headed off ECE from questions of oil and atomic energy.

One important feature of the ECE has been the independence of its secretariat, particularly in the fact that its reports on economic questions are issued on its own responsibility and do not

[1] On ECE, see David Wightman, *Economic Co-operation in Europe* (London, 1956).

have to be agreed upon by participating Governments. It has therefore been suggested that the evident decline of its authority in recent years has been due, in part, to a paucity of good economists in the lower levels of the organization, apart from its British and American staff.

In the case of Britain, formal responsibility for handling relations with the ECE is, of course, governed by the fact that ECE is part of the United Nations and therefore comes under the Foreign Office. Since, however, the matters dealt with by ECE involve a wide range of government departments, matters relating to the delegation have been handled by an interdepartmental committee upon which all interested departments are represented. Until 1956 the chairmanship of this committee was held by the Foreign Office representative. Between 1956 and June 1958 the committee was under the chairmanship of the Treasury representative but at the latter date the chairmanship reverted to the Foreign Office, in the person of the Superintending Assistant Under Secretary in charge of the economic departments.

It is generally agreed that little importance has been attached in Whitehall to the operations of ECE and that the minimum amount of representation has been maintained. If it has not been altogether abandoned, this is only because of the possibility of a future change in the political climate which might make it desirable to make use of an existing framework for European economic co-operation in which the Soviet bloc is represented. This negative attitude has come in for some criticism on the part of those who believe, for instance, that ECE might be an independent source of assistance for certain of the Soviet satellites, but this is a question of policy upon which comment here would be out of place.

CHAPTER 2

Britain and the Crisis of Europe

THE machinery for dealing with major questions of economic policy with which Britain confronted the emergency of 1947 was largely a legacy from the war years. At this time a dominating position was held by a committee of the Cabinet presided over by the Lord President of the Council. At the official level there were a number of committees whose work was co-ordinated by a Steering Committee under the chairmanship of the Permanent Secretary to the Treasury.[1]

In the early part of 1947 two further ministerial committees were set up, one to deal with overseas economic policy and one with home policy, the latter under the Lord President.[2] On March 29th the appointment of Sir Edwin Plowden as Chief Planning Officer was announced, and in May a Central Economic Planning Staff came into being under his direction. The Planning Staff was concerned with long range questions of economic policy and with co-ordinating urgent matters of current importance, where these affected several departments at a time. In this case, the Planning Staff would provide neutral chairmen of inter-departmental committees. This apparatus was additional to that already functioning in the economic departments themselves and in the Economic Section of the Cabinet Office, which was concerned with following events in the economic sphere both at home and abroad.

In July 1947 an Economic Planning Board was set up. The director of the Economic Section of the Cabinet Office was a member of the Steering Committee and of the Economic Planning Board. He and his senior assistants were also members of

[1] Chester, op. cit., pp. 341 and 356.
[2] D. N. Chester in G. D. N. Worswick & P. Ady (eds.), The British Economy 1945–50 (Oxford, 1952), Chap XV, 'Machinery of Government and Planning'.

34

other committees dealing with economic matters, and in some cases a member of his staff acted as their secretary.

This machinery was constructed and modified at a time when it looked as though Britain would be thrown largely on her own resources. For it is fairly clear that the initiative for the Marshall Plan came from the other side of the Atlantic.[1] As early as January 1947 alarming reports of the condition of the British economy had reached the State Department, and these were confirmed by the publication on January 20th of the British White Paper.[2] In the following month there came the news of the British decision to abandon their responsibilities in Greece and Turkey. A number of consultations were set on foot within the American governmental machine, looking towards a form that American intervention in this situation might take. On the other hand, there seems no available evidence of American consultation with the British or other European governments prior to the speech given by General Marshall at Harvard on June 5th. Indeed, the fact that he was going to make a far-reaching offer seems to have been an unusually well-kept secret by Washington standards. There have been various dramatic accounts of the receipt of the news in London, but it looks as though steps were taken to see that the importance of the offer was made clear to the British Foreign Secretary as soon as possible.[3]

Once the news of the offer reached London, the machinery for exploiting it was rapidly put into action. Since it was evident that the Americans looked at the problems as one affecting Europe as a whole and not just Britain, any action involved some form of agreement between Britain and her continental neighbours. The first step was to send a member of the Economic Planning Staff to Paris to discuss the line to be taken with the French Foreign

[1] It is unnecessary here to go into the history of the origins of the Marshall Plan, upon which a number of important studies have been written: see in particular Joseph M. Jones, *The Fifteen Weeks* (New York, 1955); H. B. Price, *The Marshall Plan and its Meaning* (Cornell University Press, 1955); W. C. Mallalieu 'The Origins of the Marshall Plan', *Political Science Quarterly*, December 1958.

[2] *Statement on the Economic Considerations affecting Relations between Employers and Workers* (Cmd. 7018).

[3] The impression given by Francis Williams in his *Ernest Bevin* (London, 1952), pp. 264–5, that Marshall himself had no far-reaching plan in mind and that Bevin seized the initiative so as to turn a very general expression of interest by the Americans into a precise offer of assistance does not seem to be borne out by American sources.

Minister. The choice of an emissary from the Planning Staff, rather than from the Foreign Service, shows the Foreign Secretary's appreciation from the beginning that the operation was one which would require the full co-operation of the Treasury. Nevertheless, the first hurdles were diplomatic ones, since the acquisition of French support for co-operative action was necessarily followed by negotiations with the Russians to see whether they would agree to a scheme covering Europe as a whole. The failure to reach agreement was followed by the Anglo-French invitation to all European countries who were ready to co-operate to join with them in preparing a report for the Americans on the resources and needs of Europe during the next four years. Owing to Soviet hostility to any co-operative plan, the countries of Eastern Europe were prevented from taking part in this work, and the Committee of European Economic Co-operation, set up to draft the report, represented the first joint action of the Western European countries as such.

The CEEC began work in Paris on July 16, 1947, under the chairmanship of Sir Oliver Franks, who had with him a strong UK delegation which was ultimately about fifty strong. The British contribution of ideas and experience to the whole operation was of major importance. The report had to be ready by September 1st, and to cover the whole range of European economic affairs: production; internal financial stability; the balance of payments; the freeing and increasing of trade, with special attention to the cardinal factors in recovery: food and agriculture; fuel and power; iron and steel and transport. But the scope was even further extended while the work was proceeding; some indication of its scale can be given by the fact that the general report covered 86 large quarto printed papers and the technical reports another 350 pages.

The British Government's task of keeping contact with the European Governments participating in the planning of European recovery, was made easier by the fact that Bevin's choice of a member of the Economic Planning Staff to represent him in Paris, meant that he had someone there with easy access at home to both the Foreign Secretary and the Chancellor of the Exchequer, so that rapid decisions could be secured when required. Nevertheless more formal machinery was required. It must be remembered that in the period 1947–9 there were two aspects to the international economic work in Whitehall—the multilateral work set on foot by the Marshall Plan and bilateral country-by-country negotiations. The latter was looked after by inter-departmental committees supervised by an Overseas Negotiations Committee, set up in September 1947, with a member of the Economic Planning Staff as a 'neutral', i.e. non-departmental, chairman. Some of the delegations for particular negotiations were led by a member of the foreign service, others by someone from the Treasury or Board of Trade. The easy inter-departmental relationships with no serious worry over precedence, which were to be typical of the new period, were thus not simply the product of the demands of the new type of multilateral negotiation, though they were crucial to the latter's effectiveness.

The work on European recovery faced Whitehall with two separate problems. In the first place, the UK delegation in Paris had to be kept briefed with respect to the general lines along which Britain hoped to steer the whole aid operation. Secondly, it had to see that the UK's own role was safeguarded, work out the UK economic programme for the next four years, and decide what aid was needed and what resources the UK could itself contribute to the general programme.

For these purposes an interdepartmental committee was set up early in July 1947 (the so-called 'London Committee' for European Economic Co-operation) under Treasury chairmanship, with representatives from the Foreign Office, the Board of Trade, the Ministries of Food, Agriculture, Fuel and Power and Supply, and of the Economic Planning Staff and the Economic Section of the Treasury. Other departments concerned were associated with the work of the committee as required. Its secretariat was a mixed one, drawn partly from the Treasury and partly from the Cabinet Office.

The speed with which this committee was set was an indication once more of the importance attached by the Government to the Marshall Plan and the persons initially selected to serve on it were regarded as outstanding in their several fields. Part of the enthusiasm no doubt arose from the hope that the Marshall speech meant a new era of Anglo-American co-operation. In fact, the Marshall Plan period was to prove one of close Anglo-American intimacy, though in a different setting to that of wartime.

It was inevitable that the Americans should find the British their principal partners in their new European policy, both on the economic and on the defence side, and this may have served to hide for some time the differences of outlook that still persisted. The Americans were consistently more enthusiastic for the idea that Western Europe should be regarded as a whole, and pressed in the early stages for more elaborate and far-reaching international machinery than the British deemed desirable.

From the point of view of British Governmental organization, the setting up of the London Committee was important, in that its basic structure has remained unchanged throughout the successive phases of British relations with the European economic institutions. On the other hand, there was nothing unusual about the method adopted; what was new was rather the gravity of the issues involved, both immediate and long-term, and initially, the speed at which it was required to operate. The original purpose was to find a sound basis for once-and-for-all American aid programme, and Treasury leadership was thus natural.

The Committee was originally responsible to the Lord President of the Council, who was at the date of its setting-up still the chief ministerial co-ordinator of economic policy, but it was not part of the Economic Planning Staff. Formally the committee was regarded as a sub-committee of the Economic Steering Committee, and as the counterpart to the committee dealing with the bilateral economic negotiations.

The differences of approach between the British and the Americans revealed themselves in a number of discussions between representatives of the US Government and the CEEC in Paris.[1] The Americans insisted upon a downward revision of the committee's original estimates of the aid required, and proposed far-reaching measures of integration. The idea of a European customs union appealed particularly to certain members of OEEC, notably France and Italy. Ultimately a compromise was reached; it was agreed, in deference to British objections, that the central organization for handling the recovery programme should be merely consultative; and in lieu of a firm commitment to eliminate trade-barriers in Europe, it was agreed to set up a Customs Union Study Group.

[1] On the economic background, see R. G. Hawtrey, 'The Economic State of Europe' in P. Calvocoressi, *Survey of International Affairs*, 1947–8 (London, 1952).

The CEEC report was accepted by the governments on September 22nd and transmitted to Washington. A further period of international negotiations now followed to clear up the outstanding points of difference about the duration of the programme, and the nature of the organization to be set up. The Dutch and Belgians, for instance, hoped that two years would be sufficient to get over the effects of the war upon their economies, while the French wanted a four year period in which they could rebuild their trade and industry and make new capital investments. The Dutch and Belgians also required some persuasion that the French were not aiming at a new European hegemony through some form of permanent economic organization. Britain took an important share in the negotiations in the winter of 1947–8, during which these differences and others were ironed out. A British diplomat accompanied by M. Robert Marjolin, then Deputy Director under Jean Monnet of the French Plan and subsequently to be the first Secretary-General of OEEC, toured the European capitals early in the new year to seek out common ground. Finally, agreement was reached in time for President Truman's signature of the European Recovery Act on April 2, 1948, and the signature of the convention setting up the Organization for European Economic Co-operation on April 16th.[1]

The CEEC report in September had envisaged an organization of a temporary character only, though some people sapiently realized that such an organization once set up was likely to endure—international organizations have a way of ensuring their own survival. By the time the convention was signed in April it had been agreed merely that the organization should be set up for three or four years and that its future should then be reconsidered. The basic shape of the organization was also settled during the winter talks. The original American idea, supported by the French, would have given considerable executive authority to the Secretary-General. The compromise which was reached gave the permanent staff some powers of initiative, but made it clear that the executive power was wholly that of the participating Governments.

At this time, it is probably true to say that there were few enthusiasts in Whitehall for European integration for its own

[1] On OEEC see Eric Roll, 'Ten Years of European Co-operation', *Lloyds Bank Review* (April 1958).

sake; but it was realized that the setting up of OEEC marked a new step forward in the technique of economic co-operation between Governments, and that Britain, thanks in part to her wartime experience, was in a good position to make the best use of it.

By the time the OEEC came into being, the machinery for handling these matters in Whitehall had undergone considerable changes. In the summer of 1947 a group of University economists had prepared for the Board of Trade a report on the measures that would be necessary if the multilateral pattern of world trade and payments envisaged at Bretton Woods, and in the American loan agreement of December 1945, should show signs of breaking down. The convertibility crisis in August, and the suspension of convertibility in the following month, when British gold reserves were at a critically low level, made a move towards bilateralism inevitable. As we have seen, a special interdepartmental committee to supervise bilateral negotiations was set up in September.

On September 29th it was announced that Sir Stafford Cripps would leave the Board of Trade to take up the new post of Minister for Economic Affairs. He was to have no department of his own, only a small personal staff, but would take over the Economic Planning Staff from the Cabinet Office. The chairman of the committee dealing with the bilateral negotiations would be responsible to the new minister and not to the Lord President. The new Minister of Economic Affairs would be chairman of a new Cabinet Committee dealing with production and related matters. The two committees for home and overseas economic policy, set up earlier in the year, were now removed from the sphere of the Lord President and replaced by a single ministerial committee, with the Prime Minister in the chair, known as the Economic Policy Committee, and including the Minister for Economic Affairs, the Lord President and the Chancellor of the Exchequer.

At this point, it seemed as though the Whitehall arrangements for economic planning, including its overseas aspects, might take the form of a Ministry of Economics quite separate from the Treasury, as in certain continental Governments, and that this would provide the permanent home for the various pieces of governmental machinery in this field whether inherited from wartime or newly improvised. Whether, given the special position of the Treasury in the British system, this could have long endured, was not put to the test—but for reasons, at least in part, quite fortuitous. The 'budget leak' in November brought about the resignation of the Chancellor of the Exchequer and with so grave a crisis in the country's economic affairs, the Prime Minister's choice of a successor was clearly limited. The announcement of the appointment of Sir Stafford Cripps to the Chancellorship included the statement that the new Chancellor 'would continue to exercise the co-ordinating functions in the economic field' with which he had hitherto been charged as Minister for Economic Affairs. The effect of this was to bring within the Treasury most of the existing machinery for economic planning and co-ordination, or put another way, to ensure the final transformation of the Treasury from an organization primarily concerned with budgetary, fiscal and establishment problems into a central economic department, taking within its purview the economic life of the country as a whole. The creation in December 1947 of the new ministerial post of Economic Secretary to the Treasury may be regarded as a further recognition of the department's new role.

The new Chancellor took with him to the Treasury, as a second secretary, the chairman of the Committee dealing with the bilateral economic negotiations, but the latter's scope was now widened. He now became responsible for a whole network of official committees, dealing with the bilateral negotiations themselves, balance of payments questions, and the European recovery programme, the last of these being the 'London Committee' itself. Nevertheless, although in the Treasury, the new organization did not regard itself as being wholly of it, partly because it was felt that the earlier more limited role of the Treasury might be thought to imply some limitations upon it.

The Second Secretary responsible for this network of committees regarded himself as having a triple responsibility, to the Chancellor himself, to the Foreign Secretary and to the Board of Trade, and it was his practice to make the necessary submissions to all three and to be available to report to any one of them. Whether at this stage any question of priority arose as between the Treasury and the Foreign Office is not apparent. Once the new international machinery had been got going, the attention of the Foreign Secretary was no doubt mainly concentrated on the increasingly tense relations between the Western Governments and the USSR and upon the problems of collective defence against the Soviet threat. Given his cordial relations with the new Chancellor of the Exchequer, there was every reason for Bevin to allow him to give the lead in the economic field. Nevertheless, the formal duty of delegations abroad to report through the Foreign Office was not disputed, and since matters of foreign policy were so intimately bound up with the shape and progress of the European recovery programme, the Foreign Office had to adapt itself to the increased burden of work that this entailed. In February 1948, a new Foreign Office Department, the European Recovery Department was set up so as to relieve the Economic Relations Department of this aspect of its responsibilities.

The establishment of the OEEC in Paris as a quasi-permanent international organization and of the American Economic Co-operation Administration as the agency for distributing aid under the Marshall Plan, broadened the demands made upon the machinery of the British Government. Hitherto, a relatively small number of people had been involved, since the decisions to be made had been largely on matters of principle. Now that the European Recovery programme had to be taken into account in almost all decisions affecting the economy, it was necessary to handle the problem more broadly.

The work of the 'London Committee' was, in May 1948, divided into two, in that the task of preparing the UK programme and the submissions to be put to OEEC and to the American Government, was taken away from the 'London Committee' and handled by those responsible for the general task of determining the import programme and authorizing the expenditure of foreign exchange. Since the committee responsible for this work dealt with imports not financed under ERP as well as with those which were, its chairman was provided by the Overseas Finance Division of the Treasury.

The 'London Committee' was responsible for advising ministers on all other matters relating to ERP, and for instructing the delegation to OEEC and the Treasury and Supply delegation at Washington. Its chairman, a second secretary, continued to function in relation to the committee on bilateral negotiations in a non-departmental capacity with an under-secretary and an assistant secretary to help him. By now the idea of 'non-departmental' chairmen running operating committees of this kind was becoming established as the best method. The running of these committees was quite separate from the Overseas Finance Division of the Treasury which was responsible for the direct interests of the Treasury in such work.

The basic pattern of organization in London was continued during the years of intense activity in the international economic field that followed the establishment of ERP. The committee dealing with programmes was placed under the chairmanship of an under-secretary in charge of the general divisions, who also represented the Treasury on the 'London Committee', while the Treasury was represented on the committee dealing with the bilateral negotiations by an under-secretary in charge of the territorial divisions.

In 1950, when the pressure slackened, the inter-departmental committees were made the responsibility of a third secretary.[1]

There were also some rearrangements in 1950 at the ministerial level. In February 1950, the new post of Minister of State for Economic Affairs was created and given to Mr Hugh Gaitskell. This entailed the abolition of the post of Economic Secretary. When, however, in October 1950, Gaitskell became Chancellor of the Exchequer, the Economic Secretaryship was revived.

It was during this period that OEEC elaborated its structure and determined its methods of working.[2] The essential thing was the close partnership between the secretariat and the national delegations, which assisted the latter in their primary work of negotiating agreements between the governments. The impetus to this, at first, was given by the necessity of agreeing, as soon as possible, to a formula for the disbursing of American aid. That OEEC would be required to do this after the first quarter was suddenly sprung on the governments by the Americans. The governments were thus obliged to put up their proposals and submit them to cross-questioning by the other delegations. Later on, when in 1949–50 American aid came to be distributed on a bilateral basis, owing to a change of attitude in Washington, the

[1] For the internal organization of the British Treasury generally, see W. J. M. Mackenzie and J. W. Grove, *Central Administration in Britain* (London, 1957), pp. 312–18.

[2] See A. B. Elkin, 'The Organization for European Economic Co-operation: its Structure and Powers'. *The European Yearbook* Vol IV (The Hague, 1958).

main preoccupation of OEEC shifted to trade liberalization. The cross-questioning of the national delegations about their countries' need for aid merged into a general examination of their national economic plans and intentions. The British found that this technique was one to which their own machinery was well suited, though some had believed they could have done better at the beginning if they had been allowed to negotiate directly with the Americans. Futhermore, the British had considerable experience of such techniques, since similar methods had been used to determine the distribution of scarce national resources in wartime.

By 1950 it was taken for granted that the OEEC would remain in being and would not come to an end when the American aid programme ran out at the conclusion of the four year period which had been set for it. The high-water mark of the effort at trade liberalization may be taken as having been the setting up of the European Payments Union which was agreed to by the OEEC in July 1950. British ministers had been forced to the conclusion that the dollar situation precluded any rapid move towards multilateralism and that the best hope was to free payments, as far as possible, over a more restricted area. It was hoped that OEEC might be able to develop an area in Europe where trade would be relatively unrestricted, although this was thought of as a temporary phase and the wider view was not lost to sight. On the other hand, the British Government was criticized in Parliament for not accepting the recommendation of the Economic Commission of the Council of Europe, and of the OEEC in its second report, to the effect that the members of the proposed payments union should 'agree to consult regularly on credit policy'. The Government, it was alleged, 'insisted on taking out of the payments union every valuable suggestion for joint consultation and action on monetary matters and any form of what is generally known as international management of the union'.[1] The British Government clearly wished to retain its freedom of action with regard to credit policy, which was recognized as an essential instrument of national economic management. Exchange rates were, of course, also regarded as outside the competence of OEEC, though there had been some criticism at the way in which the announcement of Britain's devaluation of

[1] D. Eccles, 476. *H.C. Debs 5s.* Col. 1975. June 26, 1950.

the pound on September 18, 1949, had been sprung on her European associates.[1]

During the period, British influence within OEEC itself was partly exercised through the fact that the first head of the British delegation, the same official as had represented the Foreign Secretary in the preliminary talks, was chairman of the Executive Committee. At the beginning it was believed that the Executive Committee, upon which only a limited number of the members of the organization was represented, would be the effective part of the whole machine, more so than the Council where all the members would be present. This was true at first. But it did not prove to be a lasting arrangement, partly because of the jealousies of the smaller Powers unrepresented on the Executive Committee, and partly, perhaps, because the Council was the only body which met at ministerial as well as official level. An attempt to set up a ministerial consultative group parallel to the Executive Comittee failed.

The Americans had in fact wished the Council itself to be composed permanently of members enjoying ministerial rank, under the impression that that would mean that decisions could be taken more rapidly and without referring back to the national capitals. But this, while conceivable under the conditions of Presidential Government obtaining in the United States, did not take into account the nature of responsible cabinet Government as practised in the European member-states.[2]

In 1952, the British Government gave up the chairmanship of the Executive Committee and assumed that of the Council, at both the ministerial and the official level and subsequently the Council has been the dominant organ, with the Executive Committee used mainly to screen material for its decisions and for coordinating the work of the organization as a whole.[3]

But this is to anticipate; by 1952 the OEEC had undergone a most important crisis during which its very survival had once more been called into question. The reasons for this are to be found in the changes in the international scene in the latter half of 1950. By then the first stage of European recovery looked

[1] For the background to the devaluation, see 'European Economic Co-operation' by R. G. Hawtrey in P. Calvocoressi, *Survey of International Affairs*, 1949–50 (London, 1953).

[2] See PEP *European Organizations* (London: Allen & Unwin, 1959), pp. 74–5.

[3] See Robertson, *European Institutions*, pp. 34–6.

quite promising, and payments to Britain itself under ERP came to an end. But with the outbreak of the Korean war and the resulting fears that this might be the prelude to Soviet military action in Europe, considerations of trade and finance took second place to the problems of re-armament and to the way in which the economic burdens of re-armament should be met by the members of the new North Atlantic Alliance. From the summer of 1950 until the Labour Government went out of office in October 1951, the financing of re-armament was the dominant element in determining its financial and economic policies, in setting the pattern of the governmental machinery through which they had to be solved, and in Britain's relations with the international organizations involved in the recovery and defence of the West.

In the immediate post-war years, Britain's defence policy was still conditioned by the assumption that the wartime alignment of the powers would, to some extent, continue to dominate world politics. The first new commitment entered into was the Treaty of Dunkirk with France, signed on March 14, 1947. This was merely a symbolic expression of the fact that France would have Britain's support in the event of any resurgence of German militarism. It was only during the remainder of the year that the new developments in relations with the Soviet Union produced a definite change in the Government's estimates of whence danger might be expected in the future. It was the deadlock reached by the Council of Foreign Ministers at their meeting in November and December 1947, that finally brought Bevin to consider entering into political and military arrangements for Western Europe which would be supplementary to the economic arrangements heralded by the Marshall Plan.

On December 23rd, Bevin informed Field-Marshal Montgomery, then Chief of the Imperial General Staff, that he had suggested to the French Foreign Minister 'that the time had come to begin the formation of a federation or union in Western Europe, and if possible to bring the Americans into it'. These plans for Western Europe were, according to Montgomery, welcomed by President Truman and General Marshall, but they were not prepared to enter into talks looking to a wider alliance, since they felt it impossible to secure from Congress any military commitment to Europe. On the other hand, the prospects for joint military action within Europe were discussed by Montgomery and the French Chief of Staff.[1]

Nevertheless, Bevin was still hopeful that any defensive arrangements for the West would include the Americans, and when at the beginning of January he started work on a draft paper for the Cabinet on the spiritual unity of the West it was certainly not with any idea of creating a 'Third Force' in Europe —an idea which had considerable vogue among his party associates at that time.

It was not until immediately before his important speech in the House of Commons on January 23, 1948, that Bevin decided how far he should go in the direction of creating a new treaty system in Western Europe, but the speech included a statement which marked the formal adoption by the Government of a policy of collective self-defence directed against the possibility of further Soviet expansion in Europe. 'The time has come,' said the Foreign Secretary, 'to find ways and means of developing our relations with the Benelux countries . . . I hope,' he continued, 'that treaties will thus be signed with our near neighbours, the Benelux countries, making, with our Treaty with France, an important nucleus in Western Europe . . . We are now thinking of Western Europe as a unit. The nations of Western Europe have already shown at the Paris Conference dealing with the Marshall Plan their capacity for working together quickly and effectively. That is a good sign for the future. We shall do all we can to foster both that spirit and the machinery of co-operation.'[2]

The immediate achievement of the new policy was the Brussels Treaty of March 17, 1948, which was a treaty of collective self-defence with France and the Benelux countries and which, unlike the Dunkirk Treaty which had been specifically directed against Germany, referred to the possibility of an armed attack in Europe without naming the potential aggressor.

A telegram from the assembled foreign ministers to the US Secretary of State at the time of the signing of the Brussels Treaty, had expressed the hope that it would lead to a wider

---

[1] Viscount Montgomery of Alamein, *Memoirs* (London, 1958), pp. 498–9; Francis Williams, *Ernest Bevin*, p. 267; H. Truman, *Memoirs* Vol. 2 (London, 1956), p. 257.

[2] 446. *H. C. Debs* 5s. Cols. 396–7.

western association;[1] and on April 23rd the Americans received a telegram from Bevin suggesting that the US Government call a conference to discuss defence arrangements for the whole North Atlantic area.[2] Meanwhile, however, it was necessary to wait for the evolution of American political opinion, stimulated by the Communist *coup* in Czechoslovakia—an evolution whose turning point was marked by the Senate's passage of the Vandenberg resolution favouring regional arrangements 'based on continuous and effective self-help and mutual aid' on June 11th.

During this time, Western Union as the Brussels Treaty Organization was usually styled, made slow progress; its machinery was purely consultative and it in no way met the demands of those who desired some more organic link between its members. Furthermore, any building-up of actual forces had to await the British Government's decision in favour of planning for the creation of a British force for the European theatre—a decision for which the CIGS was pressing throughout the period from January to May.[3]

Bevin's hesitancies at this point, ascribed by him partly to the needs of keeping in step with the Commonwealth, were do doubt also due in part to his belief that without the Americans no serious step forward was possible, and perhaps, to the hope that the apparent intransigence of the Russians would not be permanent, and that close regional alliances might still prove unnecessary.

In any event, it is clear that the movement for uniting Europe on some wider basis on general ideological grounds which commanded support at the time on both the Labour and the opposition benches, and which reached its climax with the unofficial Hague Conference in May 1948, evoked no enthusiasm from Bevin or his closest colleagues. It was with some reluctance that the British Government went along with its partners in the Consultative Council of the Brussels Treaty Organization in their agreement in January 1949 to set up a new European body to be called the Council of Europe. And British influence was exerted

[1] Ivone Kirkpatrick, *The Inner Circle* (London, 1959), p. 205. The American Secretary of State was General Marshall at the time, not Mr Dean Acheson as given by Sir Ivone Kirkpatrick.

[2] Truman *op. cit.*, pp. 258–9.

[3] Montgomery *op. cit.*, pp. 499–502.

to see that the statute, which was signed on May 5, 1949, gave the principal authority to the Committee of Ministers acting like the Council of OEEC on the principle of unanimity, and not to the quasi-parliamentary Consultative Assembly, upon which the enthusiasts for integration placed their principal reliance.

From the point of view of the immediate political and military prospects, much more importance was attached in Britain to the negotiations which began in July 1948 with the idea of producing a treaty that should make it clear to the Russians that the United States would regard the further expansion of Soviet control in Europe as a threat to itself. The Berlin blockade helped to dramatize the issue and the North Atlantic Treaty was signed on April 4, 1949. Some of those who had taken part in the negotiations—notably the Canadians—believed that it was a mistake to concentrate merely on the immediate military emergency, and that the new Alliance would only justify itself if it were the prelude to the creation of a genuine political community. They therefore insisted upon the inclusion in the text of the treaty, a statement about the necessity for promoting conditions of stability and well-being, and the possibility of taking joint economic action for this purpose.

Article II of the North Atlantic Treaty, which embodied these proposals, meant that the dilemma before British policy was now in a sense, institutionalized. Should Britain go ahead and make the most of the new European institutions, or work for the translation into action of the North Atlantic Treaty's apparent promise of community building on a wider scale?

The development of NATO was conditioned, however, not so much by the ultimate purposes of its members, as by the pressure of external fact. The explosion of a Soviet atomic device in July 1949, and the outbreak of the Korean War in June 1950 made the United States increasingly conscious of the possibility of a direct Soviet military threat in Europe. At the same time, the American Congress was insistent, as a condition of aid, that concerted plans for meeting such a threat should be worked out, so that none of the aid given should be diverted to purely national purposes. The military liaison committees, set up under the Brussels Treaty, were expanded into something resembling a planning staff and the American observer group, which had been set up to effect liaison with them, increased the scope of its participation in their work. [1]

The first meeting of the NATO Council, set up under Article 9 of the first Treaty, met in Washington on September 17, 1949, and decided to meet in future annually at least and additionally when necessary, and that the normal representation would be at Foreign Minister level. [2] A Defence Committee of the Defence Ministers of the member countries was set up to meet annually also, and to be responsible for a unified plan of defence. Its principal military advice was to come from the Standing Group consisting of the Chiefs of Staff (or their representatives) from the United States, the United Kingdom and France, which was to be in continuous session in Washington. General guidance on policy was to be given by the Military Committee of the Chiefs of Staff, upon which all the member countries were to be represented.

From the British point of view, the machinery of NATO in its early stages had a familiar appearance. The Council might be taken as the equivalent of the British Cabinet, the Defence Committee of the Ministry of Defence, and the Standing Group of the Chiefs of Staffs Committee. The real responsibilities within NATO at this time rested with the Committee of Defence Ministers, and this fact gave the British Ministry of Defence the leading position in Whitehall in respect of relations with all branches of the Organization.

For Britain it was a piece of good fortune that the development of the Ministry of Defence in its essential aspects had already taken place—otherwise the exigencies of NATO might in themselves have demanded a comparable administrative reconstruction. The Ministry itself had come into existence in January 1947. In 1947 it took over the Chiefs of Staff Committee and its important network of sub-committees. During the war years, co-ordination between the civil authority and the military had been assured by the Chief Staff Officer to the Prime Minister, who had also held the post of Secretary to the Chiefs of Staffs Committee. When the Ministry of Defence was created, the post became that of Chief Staff Officer at the Ministry of Defence.

[1] See Roger Hilsman, 'On NATO Strategy' in Arnold Wolfers ed., *Alliance Policy in the Cold War* (Baltimore, 1959).

[2] On the successive changes in the internal organization of NATO see Lord Ismay, *NATO, the First Five Years* (Paris, 1955).

Subsequent re-organization was to emphasize the integration of the military side of the Ministry with the rest of the Department. In 1955, the Chief Staff Officer became Permanent Chairman of the Chiefs of Staff Committee, and in 1957 he received the additional designation of Chief of Staff to the Ministry of Defence.[1] This post was replaced in 1958 by that of Chief of the Defence Staff.

On the other hand, the planning of defence could get nowhere without the men and arms and the money to pay for them. At its second session on November 18, 1949, the North Atlantic Council set up a Defence Financial and Economic Committee of the Finance Ministers to report to the Council, and a Military Production and Supply Board to report to the Defence Committee. The latter took over the work of the Western Union Supply Board, established in October 1948, which had been served by a Western Union Military Supply Secretariat made up of persons seconded from the government services of the member countries. Both the new NATO bodies were given working staffs in London.

In another way, also, the work of Western Union foreshadowed that of the wider organization. This was in the common financing of permanent military installations—the 'infrastructure' programme as it came to be called. The Western Union ministers, meeting in Paris in January 1950, refused to accept the principle of common financing to which the British were at that time opposed. But at a meeting in Paris in April, the British reversed their position and the programme went forward. It was taken over by NATO in the following year.

Further co-ordination between military and economic planning was sought by the Council when in May 1950 it set up the Council of Ministers' Deputies to meet in London in continuous session, and to be served by a full-time organization composed, at first again, of specially seconded officers. The burden of rearmament after the outbreak of the Korean War gave increased prominence to the economic and financial aspects of defence, and, on October 27th, the Deputies decided to establish an economic and financial working group in Paris which would be drawn from the delegations of the member countries to OEEC. OEEC itself was by this time, of course, deeply concerned with the inflationary

[1] Mackenzie and Gcove, *op. cit.*, pp. 346–7.

aspects of re-armament. On the military side, discussions were in progress from September onwards about the need to set up a unified command for the NATO forces in Europe. A decision to this effect was taken by the Council at its meeting in Brussels on December 18th, and in January 1951 General Eisenhower took up his duties as the new Supreme Commander at SHAPE.

The force requirements for the NATO command were to be determined by the Standing Group. At the same time, in deference to the wishes of the members of the Alliance not represented on the Standing Group, who felt that their interests were insufficiently represented by the occasional meetings of the Military Committee, a new Permanent Committee of Military Representatives was set up at Washington; the United Kingdom, the United States and France were represented on this body by the members of the Standing Group.

A further reorganization of the central machinery of NATO was announced on May 3, 1951. The North Atlantic Council was to incorporate the Defence Committee and the Defence Financial and Economic Committee, thus becoming the sole body at the ministerial level. It would be a council of governments rather than of ministers, the particular ministers to attend at each meeting to be determined by the nature of the business in hand. This arrangement enhanced the position of the Deputies who were, in fact, to be the permanent working body of the Alliance. A new Financial and Economic Board responsible to the Deputies but working in Paris, and in close proximity therefore to OEEC, was set up in place of the existing committees and working groups in this field. In July the first agreement for an international budget was reached, making it possible to recruit a secretariat partially on a permanent footing.

Despite the controversy over the question of a German contribution to the NATO forces, which had been raised by the Americans in September 1950 and which was to be the focus of international controversy (and of British domestic political argument) for the next four years, the military arrangements of the Alliance made rapid progress in 1951–2, thanks largely to the successful outcome, from the Alliance's point of view, of the 'Great Debate' in the United States over the commitment of American forces to the defence of Europe. By 1952, important steps had been taken in the fields of supply and communications to make General Eisenhower's command operational. NATO on land, it could be said, 'had completed its transformation from a traditional alliance, with little more than a commitment to stand together, to its new form, an integrated coalition army'.[1] And in January 1952, discussions on the co-ordination of the Alliance's strength at sea, which had been going on since December 1950, resulted in the appointment of a Supreme Commander, Atlantic.

On the other hand, the rapid growth of genuine internationalism in the military sphere, particularly at Eisenhower's headquarters, was not matched on the civilian side of NATO where the individual points of view of the several governments were much more in evidence.[2] In part, as a British group studying the situation in 1952 observed, it was due to the fact that the NATO countries had no common foreign policy.[3] It may also be the case that the greater sense of urgency on the part of the military, and their own relatively recent experience of a high degree of international integration, made it easier for them to work to an international mandate. But the most important reason is probably to be found in the fact that the economic and political issues, raised by the prospect that the needs of the Alliance would play a dominant role in the affairs of its members for years to come, could not be separated from the most fundamental questions of national policy and so of national politics. Adam Smith's rival objectives of defence and opulence, appeared in different proportions when one seemed to be offered by the country's own institutions while the claims of the other were put forward in the name of a new-fangled international body. It was possible in August 1951 to find a cost-sharing formula for meeting, on an international basis, the expenses of SHAPE and its subordinate headquarters. But a formula for covering the increasing demands of the infrastructure programme took longer to arrive at; it was not in fact settled until February 1952. And even infrastructure was only a small part of the total burden of defence.

For the British Government, the elaboration of the NATO machinery raised problems not only in respect of British repre-

---

[1] Hilsman, *op. cit.*, p. 149.

[2] *The Atlantic Alliance* by a study group of the Royal Institute of International Affairs (London, 1952), pp. 94–5.

[3] *ibid.*, pp. 33–5.

sentation in the various bodies set up and the policies to be advocated within them, but also in respect of the co-ordination of these policies with its other vital political, military and economic concerns.

For the co-ordination of defence policy with the general policies of the administration, adequate machinery already existed. The Defence Committee of the Cabinet had a secretariat of its own, within the Cabinet Office, which was closely associated with with the secretariat of the Chiefs of Staff, now incorporated, as we have seen, in the Ministry of Defence; the records of the two bodies were, for instance, maintained and indexed on the same system.[1]

It was, however, also necessary to see that the economic aspects of defence were kept in mind; and this general problem was made sharper by the coming into being of NATO. In 1950 a committee of senior officials was set up for the purpose of co-ordinating British action within the alliance. It was under the Chairmanship of the Secretary of the Cabinet and included senior representatives of the Minister of Defence, the Chiefs of Staff, the Treasury (including representatives from the Overseas Finance Division and Planning Staff) and the Foreign Office.

The balance of departmental representation within this committee reflected the changes in the general conception of the purposes of the Alliance itself. The Secretary of the Cabinet was the original Chairman because, as the representative of the Prime Minister, he was able to view objectively various departmental interests; the Foreign Office reflected the political importance of NATO and, while the military element was always important, the Treasury was heavily involved too, especially for the period 1950–2 when the major decisions about finance had to be reached.

Even the most satisfactory machinery for the co-ordination of policy, whether at the official or the ministerial level, could not, of course, obscure the fact that within the Atlantic, no less than within the European framework, the decisions that had to be taken involved major questions of principle. It was not possible to avoid the awkward fact that if some of the country's resources were to be pre-empted by an international body, then it would be more difficult to make full use of them in the way that might,

[1] Mackenzie and Grove, *op. cit.*, p. 341.

from time to time, seem best from the point of view of the national interest seen as an undivided whole. This applied not merely to the question of commitment of particular formations or their equivalent to international commands such as SHAPE, but also to the even wider question of the kinds of forces that should be raised and the nature of their armament. What might best suit the Alliance might not seem the best decision from the point of view of a British Government which looked at its responsibilities in a wider geographical context.

A similar dilemma would confront the British Government in the economic field where once again the prescription that made most sense from the point of view of someone looking at the problems of Europe, or of the Atlantic Community as a whole, might differ from that which would be the outcome of a more direct concern with the maintenance of full employment at home, or the question of the balance of payments.

As we have seen, the British solution to these dilemmas was to trust in the power of negotiation and discussion to reduce divergencies between allied and associated countries to the point where there could be general agreement on the course to pursue. This in turn produced a tendency to look with some suspicion upon over-formal patterns of international organization and over-powerful international secretariats. The weight, it was felt, should always be on the national delegations to the international organizations, and the main role of the secretariats should be to provide the technical services to make such agreements easier.

Considerations of this kind predominated in British minds whenever it became necessary to make provision for new international organizations or to recast old ones for new duties. There was, however, yet another important constituent of the British approach and that was the British tradition of administrative economy. The nineteenth century had left to Britain a legacy of watchfulness wherever public expenditure was concerned, and this was enhanced within the British administrative structure itself by the system of 'treasury control'. As an American student of the British Treasury has remarked, 'economy, now as in the past, remains a principal purpose of Treasury control and is enforced—if that is not too strong a word for describing how the Treasury deals with departments—along with the priorities of

Government policy'.[1] It was, therefore, natural that Britain should look critically at the expenditures entailed by the new international organizations at a time of general stringency, and particularly, when they involved payments abroad. It was felt that international organizations would too rapidly come to regard themselves as indispensable and to increase the scale of their financial demands even when the work available for them to do was declining. This general British position was also to play its part when, in 1951, the time came for a review of the respective roles of NATO and OEEC in the new situation created by general re-armament and the altered nature of the American aid programme. By the US Mutual Security Act of October 10, 1951, which came into force at the end of the year, the ECA was replaced by a new Mutual Security Agency whose fundamental concern in the allocation of aid would be its contribution to military security, and, as we shall see, it was in the same year that the European Recovery Department in the Foreign Office disappeared and was succeeded by the Mutual Aid Department.

[1] S. H. Beer *Treasury Control* (Oxford, 1956), p. 15.

CHAPTER 3

The Development of the Organizations

THE development by NATO of machinery for dealing with the economic problems of re-armament had raised from early on the question as to whether it was necessary to retain a separate organization in the form of OEEC. As has been seen, NATO made use of OEEC's resources for its early work in this field, but from the beginning of the rearmament drive the possibility of the amalgamation of the two bodies was discussed at length in the British press. Despite the difficulty created by the presence of some neutral countries in OEEC, and despite the feeling in some continental quarters that it was essential to retain this organization as a symbol of the desire for greater economic unity in Europe, it would appear that British opinion was, on the whole, favourable to the idea of amalgamation. It did not appear reasonable to develop two bodies dealing with largely similar questions, particularly in view of the demands which they would make upon the relatively small number of qualified persons in the field of international economics. But the whole question was further complicated by differences of views as to where the civilian side of NATO should be permanently located. The British, and some Americans also, who attached central importance to Anglo-American co-operation, were in favour of London. But the Europeans and most Americans wished the civilian headquarters of NATO to be located as close as possible to the military authorities. Furthermore, the smaller countries resented what they regarded as an Anglo-American domination of the Alliance and were for that reason favourable to Paris.

The crucial stage began with the meeting of the North Atlantic Council at Ottawa in September 1951. It was then that a temporary committee of the Council was set up to examine the whole question of the sharing of the economic burden by the member countries of NATO. The work of this devolved upon its executive bureau, the so-called committee of 'three wise men'. The British member of this was to have been the Chancellor of the Exchequer, Mr Hugh Gaitskell, but in view of the election campaign that autumn he was replaced by a member of the Treasury, Sir Edwin (now Lord) Plowden. During the winter of 1951–2, an examination of the economic problem was carried on parallel with negotiations about the new shape to be given to the NATO institutions themselves.

The new British Government that came into office in October 1951 took the view, originally, that OEEC could be wound up and its economic functions transferred to NATO. This view was held partly because it seemed likely that there would be no further multilateral distribution of American aid, the original *raison d'être* of OEEC, and partly because of the prevailing British preference for Atlantic as opposed to European institutions. There was a fairly sharp conflict between Britain and other members of OEEC about British wishes to curtail the OEEC budget. The British did not get their way on this point, although some cuts in the budget were made. The general climate of American opinion made the idea of burden-sharing obsolete and, with the recognition of this fact, the preservation of the separate identity of OEEC became more secure. The final decisions that were to govern the main Atlantic and European organizations during the remainder of the 1950s were reached at the meeting of the North Atlantic Council in Lisbon in March 1952.

Here there had to be yet a further reconciliation of opposed views, this time on the actual shape of the new organization of NATO. The United States was successful in getting Paris accepted as the centre of NATO's activities on the civilian side. It also wished to have a strong international staff to follow up and implement the decisions made by the governments. The key person was to be the holder of the new office of Secretary General, who was to be the vice-chairman of the Council and to preside over it in the absence of the Foreign Minister whose turn it was to hold the chair. The British still unsuccessfully fought to have the headquarters located in London. They also wanted a rather different kind of organization. They did not disagree with the idea of a Secretary General at the head of an international staff with access to the Council and with the power of submitting recommendations to it. But they wished to limit the size of the staff and to have a Council which would work through two main committees—a military committee and an economic and production committee—with the Secretary General not responsible for the staff of the former. The permanent representatives on the Council would themselves elect a vice-chairman who would preside over the non-ministerial meetings.

The final form that NATO took turned out to be a compromise, but the essential unity of the Council was maintained. The fact that the British eventually provided the Secretary-General in the person of Lord Ismay, with his background of experience in the British War Cabinet machinery, might have been expected to give a rather British cast to the new form of organization.[1] He would have preferred to keep the staff of NATO to something rather like the functions of the British Cabinet Secretariat. That is to say, the staff would have co-ordinating and follow-up functions while the driving force would have come from other quarters, in this case the national delegations. The national delegations would thus have corresponded to some extent to the different Whitehall departments under the British system, maintaining their own experts for the various problems of production, logistics and so on with which the organization would have to deal. In fact matters did not work out like this—indeed rather the reverse since it was the political consultative aspect of the Council, and consequently the general politically representative character of its deliberations, that proved the most important thing. The matters that required extensive technical expertize—for instance the annual review of the military efforts of the different countries modelled to some extent upon the annual review in OEEC and the infrastructure programme—came to be the responsibility largely of the Secretariat.

On the matter of the chairmanship, Lord Ismay insisted on taking the chair at ministerial meetings when the chairman was absent and the predecent was officially confirmed in 1956 when the Secretary General was made the chairman of the Council, and a minister selected on an annual basis of rotation was given merely the largely honorary and ceremonial post of president.

It is obvious that the period between the autumn of 1950 and

[1] I have been fortunate enough to read in ms. Dr R. S. Jordan's study of the NATO Staff/Secretariat during Lord Ismay's tenure as Secretary-General.

the Lisbon meeting of NATO in March 1952 presented to the British governmental machinery a particularly difficult and complex series of problems. In view of the fact that a multilateral approach to the major economic problems of rearmament was tacitly abandoned at Lisbon as altogether too complex as well as politically unacceptable, it may be hazarded that adequate governmental machinery was not present anywhere. But even from the narrower British point of view, arrangements had to be made for pressing the British case as regards the changes in the institutions themselves and for handling the direct impact of rearmament upon the British economy, as well as the mutual aid received from Britain's allies.

The economic machinery in Whitehall was reshaped in October 1950 to cope with the new situation. All interdepartmental work related to aid between the NATO countries was brought within the scope of a single committee which brought in the Ministry of Defence and the service departments. This committee still retained a non-departmental 'independent' Treasury chairman. A subsequent rationalization completed the bringing together within its scope of all mutual-aid work, and of all the remaining work of OEEC.

At this period very strong Treasury representation on the committee was necessary. In addition to the 'independent' Treasury chairman and his own staff there were no less than three Treasury under-secretaries representing overseas finance, defence and materiel, and the central economic planning staff. The economic section of the Cabinet Office was also represented.

On the other hand, in the post-Lisbon period, work of this kind fell off. There were no new major decisions of an institutional kind to be made. American aid to Britain was reduced to a number of special items and there was a general decline in the tempo of activity as regards economic co-operation in Europe. The main OEEC operations—the original division of dollar aid, the creation of the European Payments Union and the institution of the programme of trade liberalization—were complete. There were, it is true, some substantial negotiations in the period 1952 to 1955. One of the most important was on the question of the attitude to be taken by the United Kingdom to the new European Coal and Steel Committee but this will be dealt with later.

For a full understanding of the problems before the British Government on the military as well as the economic side it is, of course, essential to appreciate the methods by which NATO functioned after the Lisbon Conference, that is to say after the North Atlantic Council of the ministers, usually working through their permanent representatives at the NATO headquarters, became the central directing body.

In this period the ministers of defence and the military committee met infrequently; and after General Bradley retired from his post as chairman of the American Joint Chiefs of Staff in August 1953 the Standing Group in Washington also receded somewhat into the background. On the other hand there was a rise in the status of the supreme commander in Europe. He had received a directive from the Standing Group upon his appointment which included the authorization for him to communicate directly with individual Governments. This form of contact became of increasing importance in welding together the policies of the Alliance.[1]

The period of intensive rearmament which began after the outbreak of the Korean War came to an end in 1953–4, and the new policy adopted was that of the so-called 'long haul'—that is to say the idea of reaching a certain plateau of armaments, after which all that would be necessary would be to maintain the level attained.

The central feature of NATO's activities had become the annual review of each country's defence effort. This was important not only as a means of bringing friendly pressure upon laggards, but also as a way in which the military and civilian officials in the different countries acquired a detailed acquaintance with the needs and procedures of the central organization. The handling by the different countries of their defence problems was naturally affected by their having to expound them to a general audience. 'In this respect,' wrote the Secretary-General in 1954, 'it is stimulating to see how countries have adapted their modes of work to meet the demands of the annual review. Mention has already been made of the question of common definitions of defence activities; these are, of course, used in the review itself,

---

[1] Field-Marshal Montgomery as the deputy to the supreme commander was notified of the existence of this directive on March 12, 1951. Field-Marshal Montgomery *Memoirs*, p. 513.

but they are gradually being adopted for general use. Methods of accounting for defence expenditure, to fit in with the definitions and the timetable of the review, have been evolved, and countries have readily exchanged ideas with each other and with visiting teams from the International Staff on these matters. As staff changes take place, both in NATO itself and in national administrations, the number of officials with experience of this type of co-operative work and with a broad international outlook is steadily increasing.'[1]

At this period Lord Ismay was emphasizing the importance attached to building up in Europe a sound industrial basis capable of expansion for military purposes in an emergency. He argued that a considerable degree of burden sharing was in fact taking place within NATO not through a single formula but through such things as the stationing of units of one country on another's territory, co-operation in training, an effective sharing of infrastructure costs on an agreed formula, the defence support assistance, that is to say, financial assistance from the United States, and the supply of military equipment to the European allies from both the United States and Canada. The total cost of the joint defence effort was, for this reason, very much less than what each individual country would have to spend if it were to try to attain a comparable defensive strength. These rather optimistic conclusions did not, of course, take account of the very severe political strains that had been imposed upon the alliance by the American pressure to secure a measure of German re-armament as a contribution to the common Western defence effort. One of the main political developments of the period was the progressive ending of the occupation regime in Germany. This enabled her to be represented in OEEC by a bizonal delegation in 1948 and by a representative of her new government at the end of 1949. But there could be no question at the beginning of Germany's being a member of NATO, and, indeed, this may have been one of the principal reasons against the amalgamation of NATO and OEEC in the 1950–2 discussions.

The first move in the direction of a more unified military structure for the European countries themselves had come in August 1950 when, in the Consultative Assembly of the Council

[1] Lord Ismay, *The First Five Years*, p. 97.

of Europe, Sir Winston Churchill and M. Paul Reynaud proposed the creation of a unified European army responsible to a European defence minister and subject to democratic parliamentary control. This somewhat vague proposal produced no concrete results and what gave urgency to the matter was the new American initiative early in the autumn. The result of this was the French proposal, announced on October 24, 1950, for the creation of a European defence community under whose aegis German contingents might be enrolled without the resurrection of a national German army.

A conference to work out the details of such a defence community was convened in Paris in February 1951 and discussions continued for most of the rest of the year. It early became clear that the British, who were represented in the discussions, would be unwilling to surrender control over their national forces to a supranational authority. It was, therefore, only the foreign ministers of the six countries which had negotiated the Coal and Steel Community in the year, that is to say, France, the Federal German Republic, Italy and the Benelux countries, who affirmed their intention to set up the European defence community with specific supranational institutions.

The British Government was favourable to an initiative of this kind on the part of its continental neighbours, but the new Home Secretary, Sir David Maxwell-Fyfe, representing the British Government in the Consultative Assembly of the Council of Europe told that body on November 28, 1951, that it was quite unrealistic to expect Great Britain to join a European federation, which seemed to be the upshot towards which the moves of the six countries were tending. He held out hope only of some form of British association with such a community.[1]

During their visit to Paris in the following month, the Prime Minister and the Foreign Secretary expressed Britain's encouragement for the proposed European Defence Community and promised that British forces would be retained on the continent. Britain would be associated as closely as possible, they said, with the EDC at all stages of its political and military development; and they hoped that the countries concerned would come to an agreement to set it up. The British forces on the continent under

[1] Council of Europe Consultative Assembly, Third Session, second part, *Official Report*, pp. 512–16.

the NATO command would be linked with the proposed European army for training, supply and operations.

In the view of the British observer on the committee which drafted the proposed defence community, there were conflicting views among the continental countries as to what was desirable as regards Britain. The Dutch and Belgians were nervous of the project unless Britain took part, and constantly urged that British membership should be sought. The French, on the other hand, under the inspiration of Jean Monnet and with the experience of the Schuman plan negotiations behind them, were opposed to British membership because they thought that this would mean a watering down of the supranational idea. Despite Britain's desire to make a measure of German rearmament possible, and the American pressure exerted to this end, Britain was reluctant to surrender sovereign powers. The British did offer certain undertakings (which were less binding than those which they were ultimately to accept in the WEU agreements) but they were not acceptable to the French, and the treaty itself was signed without British participation.

Britain was not concerned directly with the question of the ratification of the European Defence Community Treaty which led to a long drawn out political struggle in France. In the end, however, when France failed to ratify, Britain took the initiative and in August 1954 secured the conclusion of the London and Paris Agreements setting up the Western European Union—an expansion of the original Brussels Treaty Organization. Not only was the new organization not supranational, but with the collapse of the EDC went the hopes of the draft treaty for a European political community which had been planned by the six countries as the next step on the road to a European federation. Nevertheless, it could be argued that the London and Paris Agreements involved a certain shelving of British sovereignty, in so far as there was now an international undertaking not to remove British troops from the continent except by agreement. The other precise undertaking by Britain was to co-operate in maintaining restrictions on the level of German rearmament, though the importance of this diminished over the years.

Later on a new field of activity emerged in WEU—that of dealing with the co-ordination of arms production in certain directions, for which the smaller and more intimate machinery of

WEU seemed more suitable than the larger NATO framework. WEU, of course, inherited the cultural activities of the Brussels Treaty Organization, but these were later absorbed by the Council of Europe. Finally, Britain acquired membership in a new parliamentary assembly, that of WEU which, unlike the Assembly of the Council of Europe, was competent to discuss questions of defence.

The change in British military policy, which was made public in the Defence White Paper of April 1957 (Cmnd. 124), involved a reduction in British forces in Europe. The treaty position was that Britain required to get a majority agreement of the WEU Powers; and the WEU Council itself was required to take the advice of the Supreme Commander in Europe. There was also a requirement that the NATO Council should be informed, though its acceptance of such a decision was not necessary. Despite the feelings which the British change of policy occasioned, and which were voiced in the WEU Assembly, there was little friction in NATO, since the NATO Council was brought fully into the picture in a discussion at which the Supreme Commander was present. Britain was, therefore, not in a position of having to ignore a formal resolution of the Council of WEU, though a compromise on the timing of the reductions and the numbers of the troops left on the continent was agreed to. It might, of course, be argued that the British precedent of 1957 was an unfortunate one from the point of view of furthering the integration of the allied forces in Europe, and that this might help to exonerate the French Government in connection with its own more independent line in NATO from 1958 onwards. But this is clearly a political question which has no direct connection with the actual machinery of the Alliance.

In 1957, when the Standing Armaments Committee of WEU was beginning to do useful work as a clearing house for discussions on research and development, and as a bridge between the United Kingdom and the continental members of the organization, the Americans made several attempts to bring the Committee directly into NATO. The British were not anxious for this because WEU already contained all the countries in Europe with research and development programmes of their own. The question was got round by inviting the Americans and the Canadians to send observers to the Standing Armaments Committee whenever they felt it appropriate. It was also arranged that concrete proposals which emerged from the WEU discussions should be circulated to the other NATO members and that projects which had gone beyond the exploratory stage should be transferred to NATO itself.[1]

The concept of intimate political consultation upon all questions affecting the interests of the Alliance as a whole was obviously weakened when, in 1956, Britain and France felt unable to consult the North Atlantic Council about the problem created by the Egyptian seizure of the Suez Canal. Some felt that consultation should have taken place despite the fact that the area concerned did not fall within the geographical sphere covered by the Alliance. An impetus in the direction of deepening and extending consultation may have been an indirect result of the crisis, since it had shown the dangers to the whole western world of important clashes between members of the Alliance, whatever their origin. This feeling was exploited by M. Spaak who succeeded Lord Ismay as Secretary-General of NATO in May 1957. By the appointment of someone politically committed to the whole idea of western integration, the Council appeared to have chosen to provide for itself a new source of political leadership within the organization. It is possible, however, that this decision was not arrived at quite in this fashion, since Spaak was not the only candidate. The position was refused by Lester Pearson, the former Canadian Foreign Minister, and the proposal for a Norwegian Secretary-General was unwelcome to members of the Alliance whose interests lay primarily in the Mediterranean. The Norwegian candidate, M. Lange, would probably have continued to act along the lines that Lord Ismay had laid down as appropriate. Pearson would probably have been rather more political in his approach than Ismay, but less so than Spaak was to prove.

Nevertheless, there was a general feeling that the initial function of building up a military machine to halt further Communist aggression was now well in hand, and that it was desirable to sustain or even create popular support for the Alliance by emphasizing its non-military potentialities. Before the Suez crisis, that is to say as long ago as May 1956, the Council had set up another committee, again known as the 'three wise men', Pearson, Lange

[1] This question is further discussed in Alastair Buchan, *NATO in the 1960s*.

and Signor Martino of Italy, in order that they should 'advise the Council on ways and means to improve and extend NATO co-operation in non-military fields, and to develop greater unity within the Atlantic community'. This Committee proceeded by way of questionnaires to the member governments and subsequently heard the representatives of these governments in person. The British Government was represented by the Minister of State for Foreign Affairs who was questioned by the Committee at a meeting on September 18, 1956. The Committee's own report was submitted to the December meeting of the North Atlantic Council.

The reply of the United Kingdom Government to the questionnaire may be regarded as an authoritative statement of the general views held by the Government as to the desirable scope of NATO at that time. The Government accepted the principle that the Council should be informed about political developments in any area that significantly affected other members of the Alliance, but they pointed out that there were difficulties in the Committee's suggestion 'that member governments should endeavour not to make political declarations significantly affecting the Alliance or its member nations without prior consultation through the Council'. It was pointed out that this might seem to prevent a member of a government of one of the allies from making any public speech or parliamentary statement on any matter which might affect an ally, without getting clearance in advance for his speech from the North Atlantic Council. Questions of timing alone made this procedure inapplicable.

On the question of widening the scope of consultation within NATO, the United Kingdom Government emphasized the necessity for care in selecting the subject matter upon which it was desired to obtain a common view. It was unrealistic to think one could get a common view of all matters. Precise rules for the choice of subject matter for consultation could not be settled in advance. But they suggested that it would be broadly acceptable if questions relating to the nature of the threat from the Communist Powers and such things as disarmament were discussed. Questions affecting the internal strength of the Alliance and its capacity for facing the Soviet strength were also suitable. The British Government's reply seems to have been affected by two main considerations. In the first place, it emphasized that national governments must ultimately retain final responsibility for their national policies for which they would, after all, be answerable to their parliaments and electorates. In the second place, the British were opposed to making the obligation to consult automatic, and to agreeing in advance to accept any advice given by the Council. The British Government also held that a government should be able to tender advice without necessarily sharing in the responsibility for the policy ultimately adopted.

With regard to disputes between members of the Alliance, the British view was that NATO's part should be limited to what diplomats call 'good offices' unless the parties were agreeable to some more formal machinery. It was not the business of NATO as such to recommend solutions for problems arising between its members, nor could it constitute itself into an executive agency in this respect.

The British Government was prepared to accept proposals designed to make the Council's procedure more effective. For instance, it favoured increasing the number of restricted sessions at the level of the permanent representatives, and also providing machinery to enable the Council to meet at short notice at any time. They thought it desirable to have Council agenda circulated further in advance of the meetings, so as to give the permanent representatives more opportunity to seek guidance from their home governments. The British Government emphasized the fact that if the desirable frankness were to be obtained at meetings of the Council, it would be essential to tighten up the security procedures in each country, so that both the instructions to countries' permanent representatives and their own reports could be kept private. No information, in the British view, should be given to the press without the unanimous agreement of the Council.

The Council, in the British view, should separate in its discussions the major political issues from military and administrative ones, and should develop a more orderly method of selecting and preparing the political questions to be discussed. They recommended as a model for this purpose the existing Working Committee on Soviet Affairs. A deputy Secretary-General or assistant Secretary-General for political affairs should be made chairman of a working group whose business it would be to keep in touch with the national delegations, and see that the political questions they wished to have discussed were previously reviewed by it. It is obvious, once more, that the model of the role of the Cabinet Office was very much in British minds at this time. It was thought desirable that ministers should be able occasionally to attend meetings of the Council which were, nominally, at permanent representative level. Finally, on the question of the Council it was not thought that it needed to increase the amount of ex- pertize directly available to it in the Secretariat itself.

The British view was that the meetings of the Council should normally be presided over by the Secretary-General. They did not wish to limit his functions by setting down hard and fast rules, but felt that caution should be exercised if he adopted the role of mediator between members. It was also pointed out that the British had already contributed to making political consulta- tion more effective by giving instructions to their permanent representative which would enable him to make position state- ments on their behalf with regard to general questions of foreign policy. The question of an economic role for NATO, which had been in abeyance since 1952, was raised again by the questionnaire, and was, indeed, to become of increasing impor- tance in subsequent years as opinion generally came to attach more importance to the Soviet economic challenge and to the question of aid to underdeveloped countries which was thought of as one of the replies to the challenge itself. With regard to this question the British reply in 1956 was rather cautious. Britain would welcome co-operation between members of NATO within the more general international organizations of a specialized kind, but this should not be pressed to the point of working out specific policies which members would be committed to support- ing *en bloc*. The basic aim should remain that of reconciling conflicts which might otherwise prove destructive to the main purposes of the Alliance. The OEEC still remained, in the British view, the main forum for direct economic consultation, and the British Government itself was satisfied with existing arrangements there for consultation with the United States and Canada. They would, however, support a proposal for a working party of OEEC itself to consider the further development of its relations with the two North Atlantic countries.

The Government was not favourable to NATO extending its interest in public works from infrastructure to works built for civilian use, and thought that its relations towards aid for under-developed countries within the Alliance itself, that is to say, Greece, Turkey and southern Italy, should be limited to making a political appraisal of the problems, while leaving the actual operation of assistance programmes to other agencies. With regard to the more canvassed matter of help for underdeveloped countries outside NATO, OEEC should collect information on what the individual members were doing, so as to help assess the relative weight of Western and Soviet assistance. It was felt that any direct discussion of aid within the NATO framework would be self-defeating, because of the hostility which many of the underdeveloped countries, committed as they were to neutrality between the Great Powers, had shown towards the organization. No new agreement in this sphere should be entered into. The proposed United Nations organization, SUNFED, should be supported subject to the majority of the members of the United Nations joining in.

What was specially desirable was consultation about matters coming up in the economic agencies, where the Soviet bloc itself was represented, so that the NATO countries should not express differences of view which might be exploited to their disadvantage. The British Government was agreeable to the idea of an examination by NATO of the political and strategic implications of the work of OEEC in the fields of conventional and nuclear energy. It might also be useful to examine the economic resources available to the NATO countries in relation to the problems of competitive co-existence. For instance, one could examine their internal and external investment programmes as compared with their direct expenditure upon defence. One could also examine comparatively the activities of the Soviet bloc and the NATO countries in underdeveloped countries, and look into the matter of the reliance of the economics of certain NATO powers on oil from the Middle East, with all the political implications involved. This last point, it must be remembered, was in a document which was drawn up at a time when the Suez question was already very much on the international agenda. The British recommendations were fairly closely followed in the Committee's report, which included the following paragraph: 'It is easy to profess devotion to the principle of political—or economic—consultation in NATO. It is difficult, and has in fact been shown to be impossible, if the proper conviction is lacking to convert the profession into practice. Consultation within an alliance means more than exchange of information, though that is necessary. It means more than letting the NATO Council know about national decisions that have already been taken; or trying to enlist support for those decisions. It means the discussion of problems collectively in the early stages of policy formation, and before national positions become fixed. At best, this will result in collective decisions on matters of common interest affecting the Alliance. At least, it will ensure that no action is taken by one member without a knowledge of the views of the others.'[1]

These recommendations were, in fact, followed fairly closely once M. Spaak became Secretary General. A much greater effort than previously was made in the field of co-ordinating policies relating to the Soviet threat, and in taking into account events happening outside the geographical boundaries of the Alliance but affecting its interests.

Its work was largely the responsibility of a Committee of political advisers, under the chairmanship of an Assistant Secretary-General who was, in fact, a British national. This Committee was composed of the second ranking member of each national delegation. It met weekly and any questions of political importance to the Alliance, wherever originating, could be raised by members either at the Committee or at the Council itself. The procedure of the Committee took the form of getting a statement from the particular government as to what it proposed to do in regard to some special question, for instance, the supply of arms to a non-member State. This would be followed by a general discussion with the idea of avoiding possible disputes in the future. The agenda of the Committee would put the affairs of the Soviet area and of Yugoslavia first. Second it would discuss what was known as 'the Middle East and other areas'. Other areas meant, in fact, Africa which because of certain political susceptibilities, did not appear on the agenda in so many words. The Committee could not, of course, discuss Algeria which was specifically covered by the Alliance nor the internal affairs of colonial territories of the member States.

By 1959, when there was something of a setback again owing

---

[1] 'Non-Military Co-operation in NATO': Report of the Committee of Three, par. 42.

partly to French intransigence on certain matters arising from the failure to obtain the kind of central political directory which General de Gaulle was believed to be seeking, this machinery had made some important advances. It was possible by then for the chairman of the Committee as a matter of course to ask a particular country for information of some action that it had taken as reported in the press, and to be able to rely upon getting the information for the following meeting. This bringing of matters into the open was thought to have considerable value in preventing countries going too far along certain lines that might eventually produce unfavourable repercussions in the Alliance. The limitation was that even where a general view was arrived at about some problem external to the geographical area of NATO, it was not possible to set up NATO machinery for handling it. In the end, action was a matter for individual countries. It should be added that in the most important field of policy of all, that of relating to direct contacts with the Soviet bloc, 1959 also marked something of a retrogression since the idea of a summit meeting or of summit meetings so much canvassed in that year was looked upon with suspicion by the smaller NATO powers as likely to leave them out of proper consideration when major decisions were taken. In this case, as in others, the desirable qualities of flexibility on the one hand and maximum consensus on the other, seemed difficult to reconcile.

The British Government fully appreciated that this increase in the political activity of NATO in the period 1957 to 1959 made the staffing of its political departments a matter of considerable importance. The Secretariat had always included a number of experts on particular aspects of NATO affairs which had been of permanent interest, for instance, Soviet policy, German questions and nuclear questions. By May 1959 there were three sections of the political division of the Secretariat. In the first place there was a research section dealing with all the correspondence with the Soviet Union on disarmament and so forth. Secondly, there was a general affairs section which among other things, dealt with problems arising between the NATO countries. Finally there was a newer section which dealt with areas not directly covered by the treaty. This development also raised questions as to the proper staffing of the delegations which will be considered later. It may be noted that despite the extreme importance attached to NATO as a place where the changing aspects of the Soviet threat could be analysed, it was not thought necessary that the British delegation itself should have an expert on Soviet affairs, since it was thought possible to supply at short notice from London the necessary specialists.

The whole question of the use of such experts from the national capitals is one of considerable importance. To rely on them has one particular advantage in that it enables certain governments within NATO to discuss matters which other governments do not wish to touch. For instance, the Scandinavians do not wish to discuss Persia, and Canada does not wish to discuss African questions with colonial Powers. It is possible to ask countries who have experts on a particular problem of this kind to send them to a meeting and the others can stay away as having no suitable representatives. In the upshot a small Committee only is assembled and this can report to the Council as necessary.

The problems of recruitment to the Secretariats of international bodies themselves are outside our present scope. In NATO there is a particular difficulty in the division between those on loan from governments and those who are permanently with the organization both from the point of view of inter-staff relations and from the point of view of particular governments who have different ideas as to the extent to which their nationals should shed their home allegiance for the period of their second-ment. On the whole, the British Government seems to have appreciated the fact that it can best serve NATO by being willing to supply fully qualified persons on secondment.

There are also limitations upon what the Secretariat itself can do in the political field, arising from the fact that it has no independent sources of information. There is nothing in the organization that corresponds to the inflow of telegrams to a national foreign office, so that the British members of the Secretariat for instance feel less well informed about what is going on in the world than, for instance, their own delegation to NATO or the members of the British Embassy in Paris. This weakness has, of course, a parallel in the fact that military intelligence in NATO is also a matter for individual countries, so that the Standing Group and other military organs have to content themselves with accepting and co-ordinating what comes to them from national sources.

Britain has also been directly concerned with the two occasions upon which NATO has been active in attempting to conciliate disputes between its members. Following upon the report of the 'three wise men' the North Atlantic Council passed the following resolution on December 13, 1956. 'The North Atlantic Council: Reaffirms the obligations of all its members, under Article I of the Treaty, to settle by peaceful means any dispute between themselves; Decides that such disputes which have not proved capable of settlement directly be submitted to good offices procedures within the NATO framework before member governments resort to any other international agency except for disputes of a legal character appropriate for submission to a judicial tribunal and those disputes of an economic character for which attempts at settlement might best be made initially in the appropriate specialized economic organization; Recognizes the right and duty of member Governments and of the Secretary-General to bring to its attention matters which in their opinion may threaten the solidarity or effectiveness of the Alliance; Empowers the Secretary-General to offer his good offices informally at any time to member governments involved in a dispute and with their consent to initiate or facilitate procedures of inquiry, mediation, conciliation, or arbitration.'

The first case of this kind was Cyprus. It was taken up by the Secretary-General at the point in the dispute when the Greeks said that unless something were done they would leave the Alliance. The Secretary-General toured the capitals concerned without great success but succeeded in preventing a total breakdown. The important thing is that afterwards the whole subject was discussed as often as two or three times a week at the Council with all the other allies present as well as the three countries involved. The representatives of the other countries gradually became experts themselves; and their comments could, therefore, not be ignored. With regard to the countries directly concerned, they could not afford to walk out on the discussions since they were interested in other items on the Council's agenda. Although no solution was reached within the NATO framework, the Greeks were in a less belligerent mood by the end of these discussions; and a fortnight after NATO gave up its direct concern with the Cyprus issue, the Greeks and Turks made direct contact for the first time.

A similar procedure proved unsuccessful in the case of the

dispute between Great Britain and Iceland, but the general view came to be that, given the choice of the members of the Alliance to avoid disputes with each other, this machinery was likely to continue to be of permanent value.

British caution as to the possibility of developing the economic side of NATO was perhaps justified by the limited development in the period 1957–9. An Economic Committee met, as well as the Political Committee, but apart from questions directly concerned with defence it proved of less importance. It did not deal with the general question of the harmonization of economic politics which continued during this period to be the concern of OEEC. On the other hand, the sub-committee on the Soviet economic threat remained on the lookout for points at which the interest of the Alliance might be jeopardized by some Soviet action, and produced useful analysis of the economic situation in the Soviet Union and its satellites. It could also look outside and see what might be done to prevent the Soviet Union taking advantage of the economic embarrassment of some non-member country and there have been (naturally unpublicized) examples of action of this kind.

The British Government, in its reply to the 1956 questionnaire, showed itself not unaware of the fact that the success of NATO depends to a large extent upon the state of public opinion in the member countries. It had been decided from the beginning that NATO should not operate an information programme of its own, but should work through the information services of the member governments. Not all of these governments were equally well equipped in this field, and attempts to get some countries to improve their machinery were not wholly successful. For this reason the main point in this section of the United Kingdom's reply was the necessity for improving national information services. On the other hand, the British Government was opposed to any suggestion that NATO should set up a 'psychological warfare bureau', or an 'ideological planning staff'.

The United Kingdom Government was satisfied about the relations between the NATO information services and its own information services, but thought that there should be a periodical re-examination of the whole question. The main channel from the NATO information services to the United Kingdom has been through the British delegation in Paris, though the NATO information services have also maintained direct links with the Central Office of Information, the BBC and so on. The British Government thought that there was no need to have a special NATO information officer in the United Kingdom, but thought that the idea of such a special officer might have value in certain other member countries. It is also relevant here, and may have influenced the British view, that the activities of unofficial bodies interested in the work of NATO such as the Atlantic Treaty Association have been particularly important in Britain. The question of major political pronouncements on NATO questions is, of course, separate from routine questions of information and is more directly related to the whole question of the political framework within which the machinery of NATO is expected to operate.

The traditional British view that statements of policy should be made only by responsible ministers is, of course, difficult to apply directly to an international organization of this kind, and there have been criticisms in Britain from time to time when political pronouncements have been made by the Secretary General or the Supreme Commander in Europe. The latter has a political adviser on his staff, an American diplomat seconded to him but with access to US sources of information.

The British Government appeared to believe that it had, by 1956, developed the requisite machinery in London for dealing with the problems presented to it by NATO. It did not, therefore, feel itself obliged to act along the lines suggested in paragraph 93 of the report of the 'three wise men', which ran as follows: 'It is indispensable to the kind of consultations evisaged in this report that Permanent Representatives should be in a position to speak authoritatively and to reflect the current thinking of their governments. Differences in location and in constitutional organization make impossible any uniform arrangements in all member governments. In some cases it might be desirable to designate a high official in the national capital to be concerned primarily with NATO affairs. The purpose would be to help both in fostering NATO consultations, whenever national policies impinge on the common interest of the Atlantic Community, and in translating the results of such consultation into effective action within the national governments.'

In London it was the Foreign Office, as such, which took the lead in Whitehall in seeing that NATO affairs were given their proper consideration. The role of the foreign ministers generally had become more important in NATO and that of the defence ministers less important than in its early stages, while after the idea of burden-sharing was shelved, the finance ministers also played a less significant role. Meetings of NATO defence ministers, not attended by foreign ministers, still occurred from time to time, but at the ministerial level the Foreign Secretary had become the natural head of the British delegation, with the Minister of Defence and sometimes the Chancellor accompanying him when necessary. The general British view of how NATO worked best was consolidated in the period immediately after 1956, with an emphasis upon its utility as a general forum for the discussion of military and political ideas. On the military side particular importance was attached by the British to the impact of service in NATO upon the thinking of those British officers who had had this experience. The NATO Defence College was also considered valuable, in particular for the insight given to the students from one country of the workings of the military mind in other countries. There will have been fewer civilian officials who will have had direct experience of working for NATO, but the influence upon their outlook may, in the long run, be no less significant.

Britain does not seem to have had a particularly strong view of its own about the successive developments in the military organization of NATO. As NATO's responsibilities grew, it became necessary to have more frequent opportunities for getting views of countries who were not satisfied with the periodic meetings of the Council and the infrequent meetings of the Military Committee. In December 1950 the National Military Representatives Committee was established in Washington alongside the Standing Group of the three principal Powers. Henceforth the machinery was rather a complicated one in that a new project would have to go to the Standing Group and the National Military Representatives Committee, from there to the Military Committee, that is to say the National Chiefs of Staff meeting only once or twice a year, and finally to the Council for political approval. This machinery itself came to seem inadequate to the smaller Powers and, in 1956, the Military Representatives Committee was upgraded, its name being changed to that of Military Committee in Permanent Session. Subsequently, the Standing Group had at its meetings a representative of those members of the Military Committee in Permanent Session who were not themselves members of the Standing Group.

As we have seen, the position of Supreme Commander in Europe rapidly became of cardinal importance to the organization as a whole and a direct channel of communication, between the military authorities of the various countries and the Supreme Commander, was established through national military representatives stationed at his headquarters. They were in a position to give advance warning to the Supreme Commander as to the likely reaction of their own superiors to his proposals. This was in addition to the contacts with the Supreme Commander maintained by the permanent delegations to the NATO Council. It can thus be seen that there were a number of points in the structure at which the quality of British service representation was of very considerable importance.

Another later development in NATO was the creation, under the aegis of its Armaments Committee, of a number of working groups on particular projects limited in membership to those countries directly interested in research, development and production in relation to particular items of equipment. It may well be that developments along these lines made the British Government more favourable to the idea of an eventual merger of WEU into NATO, and some development of thinking along these lines does appear to have taken place.

But the question of rationalizing the institutional structure in Europe and the Atlantic Community has all along been as much a political as a technical one, and can best be dealt with in a political context; it is closely bound up with the question of establishing the responsibility of the executive organs of the international bodies to some form of parliamentary control. The first attempt along these lines was that made in the Council of Europe whose statute was signed on May 5, 1949. As we have already seen, Mr Ernest Bevin was, on the whole, unfavourable to this development which he thought impracticable and, to some extent, a diversion from the pressing questions of mutual defence. The result of this objection to the idea of a European political authority in which Great Britain did not, of course, stand alone, though it took most of the blame for the new institution's lack of achievements, was that the primary responsibility was given to a committee of ministers acting on the unanimity principle. The Committee of Ministers never developed into an important organ and after the first three years of the life of the Council of Europe it continued to meet mainly at deputies', that is to say, at official level. The British Government regarded the proceedings of this Committee as private and declined to give particulars of the instructions to its representatives on these grounds. This policy was reaffirmed in a written parliamentary answer on May 21, 1958, when a private member had drawn attention to answers on this matter given by the German Government in its Parliament.

The central innovation of the Council of Europe was, of course, the Consultation Assembly but, here again, Britain was largely responsible for the restrictions placed upon its competence.[1]

Once the Consultative Assembly had come into being, the United Kingdom fully co-operated in its work, sending delegations which, in the early years, were composed of parliamentarians of considerable weight at home. As far as practical action is concerned, the Consultative Assembly can only work through resolutions which the governments may or may not translate into international conventions which, when ratified, have the force of law in member States.

Great Britain was, in some respects, fairly forthcoming with regard to the conventions resulting from the recommendations of the Consultative Assembly. On March 6, 1951, Great Britain ratified, in part, the European Convention for the Protection of Human Rights and Fundamental Freedoms, which set up a European Commission of Human Rights to which any signatory could appeal if it believed that any other signatory was infringing the Convention. Great Britain was, however, not among the States which agreed to the optional clause permitting individuals to appeal to the Commission provided the States concerned had agreed to this clause. The Convention also set up a European Court of Human Rights which could deal with cases submitted to it by States when these had not been settled satisfactorily by the Commission. Great Britain was not one of the eight States whose ratification brought this part of the Convention into force in 1958. It was, however, one of the States that ratified a protocol

[1] Lord Strang, *Home and Abroad* (London, 1956), p. 290.

to the Convention regarding the rights to private property, to free elections, and to education; and it also accepted the optional declaration extending the Convention to a large number of dependent territories overseas.

Great Britain also co-operated closely in the cultural aspects of the work of the Council of Europe, through the Cultural Relations Department of the Foreign Office. Work of this kind had already begun through the Brussels Treaty Organization, some of whose work, performed afterwards by WEU, has as we have seen latterly, been in process of being transferred to the Council of Europe.

In other respects Britain's record here was less satisfactory from the European point of view. In 1957 there was a certain amount of pressure upon the Government in Parliament with regard to its failure fully to co-operate in work relating to the simplification of frontier formalities. Here the principal objection seems to have been the insistence by the Home Office that the passport was an essential document for visitors to this country, in view of the fact that there was no police registration once visitors had been admitted to the country. Although some of the apparent concessions to the idea of the freest possible movement of persons and goods (for instance, motor cars) made by continental members of the Council, may have been less drastic than they appeared on paper, it remained true, and indeed became increasingly true, that entry into Britain was more strictly and uncomfortably controlled at the ports, than entry into at any rate most of the continental countries belonging to the Council. Although administrative practice could easily explain the division for passport examination of persons coming into the country between British nationals and aliens, this differentiation was a source of uneasiness where foreign visitors were concerned, and continued to make them think of Britain as more unfriendly to the European idea than some of its more positive contributions would justify.

WEU, which was brought into being by the London and Paris Agreements in the late summer of 1954, was the other international organization of which Britain was a member and which had, among its organs, a Parliamentary Assembly. Unlike the Consultative Assembly of the Council of Europe, the Assembly of WEU can discuss and has discussed matters of defence.

There are a number of questions raised by the existence of assemblies of this kind, and by British membership of them.[1] These questions may be divided into four groups. The first of them deals with the proliferation of these assemblies in the European and Atlantic communities and with suggestions for their rationalization, so as to give them greater effectiveness and avert the overcrowding of the timetable of the national parliamentarians who, at present, have to man them. This aspect of the matter can only be dealt with satisfactorily at a later stage in the discussion, when we have taken into account the developments in the lesser Europe of the Six. The next group of questions concerns the methods by which British representation is secured, and the relations of these representatives to Parliament itself and to the British Government. The third group of questions relates to the extent to which Parliament itself is made aware of, and gives attention to, the doings and recommendations of the international assemblies. Finally there is the problem of the effect upon the constitutional responsibility of the British Parliament which membership in such organizations might conceivably produce, if the ideas of their more federal-minded members were to gain the upper hand. But this is a part of the more general constitutional question of the relations between Britain as a sovereign State and the international organizations with which we are dealing and will more appropriately find its place at the end of this study.

The members of the British Parliamentary Delegation to the Consultative Assembly of the Council of Europe and the Assembly of WEU, are appointed by the Prime Minister of the day, after consultation with the party whips, in rough proportion to the parliamentary strengths of the parties, and may include members from either House.

In considering the composition and work of these delegations, it is necessary to take into account the fact that in Britain, in contrast to certain other countries which are members of these organizations, we have a governmental system normally based upon a single majority party. The delegation thus consists of representatives of the Government and the Opposition respec-

---

[1] There is a fairly full discussion of them in the paper by J. Blondel, 'The United Kingdom', in K. Lindsay, *European Assemblies* (London, 1960), which appeared after the MS of the present study was completed.

tively and, generally speaking, the Opposition representatives will tend to be persons of greater weight, since the leading figures in the Government party of the time will normally hold ministerial office and so be unavailable usually for service on the delegation. The organization and conduct of these delegations also reflects the fact that, in Britain, there is no system of committees by which Parliament might provide for the discussion of foreign affairs in a confidential atmosphere along non-party lines. This is reflected in the conduct of the delegations, since it was noted that, at Strasbourg, the British were the only delegation to maintain separate party secretaries and separate party rooms in the Council of Europe building.[1]

These conditions of British political life also affect the extent to which the briefing of parliamentarians is possible on the matters of interest to the Government which the assemblies are likely to discuss. There is a strong British convention that civil servants avoid direct contact on political matters, except with the ministers to whom they are individually responsible. Nevertheless, within these limitations, the Government is clearly concerned to see that British MPs are adequately equipped. On the official side a member of the Foreign Office goes to the assemblies, quite independently of the political parties, and is available to give guidance to anyone who asks for it. Members of the Opposition parties ask for such guidance less frequently than Government supporters, since they do not wish to inhibit themselves from criticism. Generally speaking, they prefer to rely on party briefs though they may occasionally get background material (not policy advice) from the Foreign Office representative. The Foreign Office in turn tends to limit its own advice to stating the pitfalls which the Government is anxious to avoid and does not, on the whole, propound a positive line. But its representatives keep in touch with the secretaries of the delegations of all three parties and when the agenda is received ask them whether they require any material and tell them what briefs are available. It is also true that there is usually a minister present for part of the session of the assemblies, and he is available to Opposition MPs as well as to members of his own party. But given the conventions of British Parliamentary Government one would not expect these contacts to be close. During the three year period in

[1] K. Lindsay, *Towards a European Parliament* (Strasbourg, 1958), p. 74.

which one British under-secretary for Foreign Affairs was present at the sessions of the Council of Europe, the practice was to have at the beginning of each session a joint meeting of the representatives of the British parties at which the under-secretary would go through the business and give the Government and Foreign Office views upon the various items that were going to come up. There would then be a general discussion, but after this there were no further contacts. The leader of the Labour Party delegation would meet the other Labour members each day to discuss the work in hand and decide the line to be followed. Any necessary research was done for the Labour members, not by a Government official, but by a member of the staff of Transport House who accompanied the delegation. On the whole then it would seem fair to say that British delegations are unequally served, in that those from the Government benches are likely to be briefed in much greater detail on the official line.

On the other hand, in this as in other matters, the British attitude is very flexible and on points upon which the Government and Opposition are in substantial agreement a different procedure may well be followed. For instance, in 1959, when a question of the proposed Free Trade Area was on the agenda, a detailed confidential document setting out a large number of hostile questions likely to be put about the proposed Free Trade Area together with the Government's replies, was circulated to all the members of the British delegation to Strasbourg. It appears that it has always been the case that the interdepartmental committee organization in Whitehall concerned with the questions of foreign economic policy has been prepared to brief members of Parliament likely to take part in economic debates in the Council of Europe. The Board of Trade, on the other hand, does not give formal briefings though it may, on occasion, provide factual information to individual enquirers.

It is understandable that the Consultative Assembly of the Council of Europe and the Assembly of WEU should have, from time to time, felt a considerable degree of frustration because of the difficulties of ascertaining the precise impact of their debates and resolutions upon the policies of member countries and, in particular, upon the discussions in their own Parliaments.

The British problem is again a peculiar one in this absence of any committee on foreign affairs. For instance, the texts of the recommendations of the WEU Assembly regularly go to the committees on foreign affairs of other parliaments, while there is no appropriate recipient for them in Britain. On the other hand, the parliamentary question, which is highly developed in Britain, does provide opportunities for fairly frequent prodding of the Government by members on points in the proceedings of the assemblies in which they are interested.

The Council of Europe itself appointed a working party on relations with national parliaments on October 25, 1956. This committee received information on this question from the British Government on February 5, 1957.[1] In its first annual report Britain was singled out along with Germany, as one of the two countries in which most effort had been made to secure parliamentary knowledge of the Consultative Assembly's recommendations. 'In the House of Commons,' said the report, 'question after question has been put to ministers within whose competence the points raised by any given Assembly lie, and the increased awareness of the work of the Assembly thus produced in the minds of the ministers represents a considerable achievement.' There are, of course, a very large number of members of the House of Commons at any one time who have had experience in the Council of Europe in particular. This is partly because the British have an exceptionally high turnover in their delegations, it having become the custom for Labour members to serve for two years and Conservative members for three.[2] In putting such questions and, of course, in debate, the members speak as individuals, since it is as individual parliamentarians that they represent Britain in the Assemblies. As Sir Winston Churchill told the House of Commons in May 1953, there can be no question of the delegation as a whole reporting to the House.[3]

The whole question was discussed in a debate in the House of Commons on a private member's motion on February 8, 1957, which ran: 'that this House recognizes the important role international parliamentary assemblies have to play in the development of European co-operation, and considers that this can be most effectively fulfilled in the Council of Europe where parlia-

[1] Council of Europe. AS/PN/WI (8) April 1957. Procedures for bringing texts adopted by the Consultative Assembly before national parliaments.
[2] Lindsay, *op. cit.*, p. 26.
[3] Lindsay, *op. cit.*, p. 68.

mentarians could meet to discuss any aspect of Western co-operation and union'. This motion was adopted without a division.

Much of the debate concerned the necessity for bringing to-gether in a more coherent form the disparate organizations con-cerned with the progress of European unity, but there seemed general agreement among the large number of members who had taken part in the Consultative Assembly of the Council of Europe that its activities were of value.

The Assembly of WEU also set up a working party to look into the question of the extent to which governments had carried out the recommendations of the Assembly. Its rapporteur re-ported, in July 1958, that although the latest recommendations of the Assembly had been published as long ago as October of the previous year, the British House of Commons was the only national parliament which had directly discussed the problems selected by the Assembly for examination.[1]

From the point of view of the international organizations, parliaments are primarily a means of securing the degree of publicity they find necessary for their work, while from the point of view of the parliaments, they are mainly places where indi-vidual members can acquire some knowledge of the attitudes of their fellow parliamentarians in other countries. It is the know-ledge, in part, of the pressure on parliamentary time, which in all countries seems to limit the ability of parliament to give full dis-cussion to international topics, that tends to make the organiza-tions fight shy of concentrating on questions which require legis-lation. This point is not so relevant to Britain, because in Britain the Government is able to secure, through the operation of its normal majority, such legislation as it thinks desirable but, of course, the particular relationship between the British Govern-ment and the House of Commons has played its part in British thinking about the kind of international organizations that are desirable.

The important thing here would seem to be the complete control that the Government and Opposition between them have over the time available for debate. Little attention was given by Parliament during most of the period under discussion to foreign

[1] WEU Assembly, *Proceedings*, Fourth Ordinary Session, first part, July 1958, Assembly documents, Document 14, p. 172.

economic policy, as compared with foreign policy in the more general sense. And it has been argued that successive Governments were unwilling to expound these questions to Parliament in detail because they were afraid of running into difficulties. On the other hand, the committees of the separate political parties in the House of Commons had appeared to have taken a fairly active interest in matters of this kind, and to have sought for more information than was made available to them in debate. This would suggest that the level of parliamentary interest has been higher than a study of Hansard might suggest.

In addition to the Consultative Assembly of the Council of Europe and the Assembly of WEU, which are formal bodies established by treaty, there has been discussion of the idea of a further body of parliamentarians to play a similar role in regard to NATO. The North Atlantic Treaty made no provision for a parliamentary component of the organization and would probably have run into difficulties with the American Congress anyhow if such an idea had been mooted at the time. But in July 1955 an unofficial meeting of NATO parliamentarians was held, and there have been several such meetings in subsequent years. Because this is an unofficial body, the invitation to the British Parliament to send a delegation comes through the Speaker and the Lord Chancellor and not through the Foreign Office. The delegations themselves are, in fact, chosen by the party whips as is effectively the case with regard to the two formal assemblies.

In its reply to the 1956 questionnaire, the British Government expressed the hope that these unofficial meetings would become an annual event, but did not think it desirable to establish any formal link between the parliamentarians and the rest of NATO, since they thought that such an assembly might wish to discuss aspects of the organization's activity unsuitable for public debate which would only complicate the work of the Council, besides adding to the proliferation of parliamentary assemblies.

It is, nevertheless, held in some quarters that these unofficial meetings have been more useful than the formal sessions of the European Assemblies. In particular, they have made it possible for parliamentarians to acquire information from the Supreme Commanders and the Secretary-General which they would not have been able to get in any other way. NATO has always got to balance between the secrecy in which much of its work must necessarily be enveloped and the necessity, at the same time, for having an informed public opinion to support it. Individual MPs and MPs in groups can, of course, visit NATO headquarters quite apart from the meetings of the Assembly of Parliamentarians—the NATO Parliamentary Conference—as it is called. It is one of the functions of the head of the British delegation to NATO to brief all MPs who come to Paris for this purpose, though it would appear that Opposition MPs do not always take full advantage of this possibility.

CHAPTER 4

Britain and Little Europe

W E have seen that the British Government was prepared to take an active part in new international institutions that were based on the principle of leaving executive responsibility to national Governments, but of incorporating institutional arrangements to ensure that the policies adopted were, as far as possible, such as would be acceptable to the other friendly countries concerned. On the economic side this was as far as either the Government would go or as Parliament and public opinion were likely to follow it. On the military side, a more radical rethinking of past positions had taken place, and the arrangements for a common command structure under NATO, as well as the precise undertakings given under WEU about the location of British forces on the continent, were substantial derogations from national sovereignty by any pre-1939 standards of comparison. Nevertheless, as we have also seen, there were people, mainly on the continent of Europe, for whom nothing short of a federal structure, with legislative and executive authority located in supranational institutions, would suffice for either the military or the economic needs of post-war Western Europe. We have already noted that despite the political attractiveness of preventing the rebirth of independent German military power, military plans along these lines had collapsed with the failure of France to ratify the EDC Treaty. This was followed by the abandonment of plans for a European political community.

We have now to go back and look at the planning in the economic field of the six countries that had accepted, in broad outline, the idea of a possible federal future for at least part of continental Europe.

What was known as the Schuman plan for a Coal and Steel Community was prepared in France under conditions of secrecy.

88

The idea was actually launched on May 9, 1950, only a day after the return of the French Foreign Minister from a series of conferences in London. The inspirers of the plan were obviously determined that British objections to supranational ideas should not, as in the case of the Council of Europe, be allowed to affect the final structure of the proposed new institutions. It was made clear to Britain that she would not be allowed to attend the proposed conference on the plan unless she accepted in advance the supranational principle. Despite a British plea for preliminary discussions to see whether some more open invitation could not be extended, this position was firmly maintained by the French.[1]

There were temporary difficulties on the side of the British Government in handling the proposal thus thrust at them, in that Bevin himself was ill in hospital, and both Attlee and Cripps were away. Herbert Morrison, who was temporarily in charge of the Foreign Office, felt that we could not go to a conference if the outcome had thus been settled in advance. This view was accepted by his Cabinet colleagues. As far as is known, the prime British objection was the constitutional or political one and no detailed consultation of the economic interests involved was entered upon at this stage. There were, however, at that time, which was of course a period of shortage, certain economic objections, at least in the short run, which would have been brought to the attention of the Government. This was particularly so with regard to coal since the plan would have prevented us from reaping the benefit of the difference between high export prices and low domestic prices. It might also have meant that we would be obliged to export coal cheaply to Europe and to make up our own needs with dollar coal. On the steel side, there was not a great deal of consultation, but we clearly did not wish to have controls over questions of the development of the industry, or questions of location which had strategic aspects. We wished, furthermore, to keep a measure of pricing freedom in other markets and especially not to risk any interference with our freedom to meet Commonwealth demands upon our steel supplies.

It appears that consideration was given to the possibility of an alternative British plan for coal and steel. According to a foreign student of these events, the British plan would have been a purely

---

[1] See the White Paper, *Anglo-French Discussions regarding French proposals for the Western European Coal, Iron and Steel Industries* (Cmd. 7970, 1950).

technical and commercial one. It would have proposed the dividing up of the European markets, economy in transport, the elimination of non-productive plant, the construction of new plant, the establishment of national and international committees and the adjustment of protective tariffs. This was a scheme which the OEEC could have taken care of. By it, each country would have retained complete control of the decisions taken by its delegates in the international committees, through which it would have functioned. This scheme was, however, never put forward, in view no doubt of the progress made by the six countries directly involved in the Schuman Plan negotiations.[1]

The British conservative delegates to the Consultative Assembly of the Council of Europe meeting in August 1950, put forward a draft proposal of their own. This, it has been pointed out, was dominated by two principles: first, that there should be a comprehensive right of veto for all the participants, and second that any of them could give a year's notice of the termination of the agreement. This was far removed indeed from the ideas of the supranationalists and the scheme met with little response in the Assembly, where it was allowed to die in committee.[2]

The whole question was debated at length in the House of Commons on June 26 and 27, 1950. The Opposition claimed that the Government's reluctance to go into the Schuman Plan negotiations had been due to its unwillingness to lose its freedom of control in respect to certain sections of the economy, since this might interfere with its planning of the economy as a whole. Given the complexion of the other Governments concerned, it was probable that socialists would be in a minority in any supranational authority set up under the proposed treaty. Finally, the Trade Unions were thought to have suggested that they had no desire to see questions of industrial relations treated on an international basis. Whatever may be thought of the relevance of these criticisms to the Government's decision, the debate is noteworthy as being the only occasion in the period when a Parliamentary Opposition attacked the Government for its unwillingness to proceed faster in the direction of European integration.

[1] Raymond Racine, *Vers une Europe nouvelle par le plan Schuman* (Neuchâtel, Switzerland, 1954), pp. 66–7.

[2] H. J. Heiser, *British Policy with regard to the Unification Efforts on the European Continent* (Leyden, Holland, 1959), pp. 41-2. This work also contains some points on subsequent British attitudes to the policies of the Six.

The six powers agreed upon their treaty setting up the European Coal and Steel Community, and giving its High Authority certain supranational powers, and the treaty itself was published on April 18, 1951. In Britain, in June, a working party of officials was set up to produce an assessment of the probable consequences for Britain if the Community came into being, and to suggest the kind of policies that Britain should adopt towards the new institutions.

The working party endorsed the decision arrived at in the previous year that, while there was much in the general purposes of the new Treaty that Britain could support, the economic advantages of full membership would be outweighed by the disadvantages. They stressed in particular the incompatibility of the obligations which Britain would incur as a member of the Community with her Commonwealth responsibilities. A crucial case of this incompatibility was the power which the high authority would have in time of scarcity to restrict exports from Britain to Commonwealth countries.

Although the working party recognized that the amount of supranationalism in the Community itself had been considerably watered down during the negotiations, full membership would still entail a considerable surrender of the Government's freedom of action to an external authority, possessed of powers over individuals and firms that it could enforce through its own legal processes without intervention by the Courts of the United Kingdom itself. To join the Community would be to take an important political decision with internal as well as external implications.

Finally, it was noted that the Treaty might prove to be only a partial implementation of the federal objectives of its sponsors. Both M. Schuman's original statement and the preamble to the Treaty implied steps towards European federation in other fields than coal and steel, which might be inconsistent with British interests. On the other hand, Britain's failure to accept these ultimate objectives might make it unwelcome as a full member of the Coal and Steel Community itself.

In these circumstances it was, nevertheless, thought desirable that there should be some permanent relationship established with the Community, and consideration was given to two alternative methods: partial membership, by which the Treaty would be subscribed to though with reservations, or alternatively, some form of association without actual adherence to the Treaty itself.

Partial membership would have to include, it was argued, special provision for the United Kingdom on the following points. There would have to be recognition of the special relationship with the Commonwealth, so that in shaping their policies the high authority and other institutions of the Community would be obliged to take these responsibilities fully into account. Britain would have to retain the right to take special measures to preserve her steel industry from being reduced by the effect of competition in a free market to a level regarded as unsafe from the strategic angle. Finally, the Community would have to accept the basic principles and general methods by which the nationalized coal and steel industries in Britain conducted their affairs. Consideration was also given to the possible need for Britain to retain control over exports of coal and steel in times of shortage. This was held to be essential during the transitional period provided for in the Treaty, but no decision was arrived at as to whether control over exports would be necessary later on.

It was felt that if these three or four points were met, the most concrete of the objections to membership would have disappeared, and it would then be a question of weighing the advantage to be derived from the influence which Britain would have in the working of the Community, as against the surviving political and psychological objections to putting our coal and steel industries under a measure of supranational control.

The form of association would be one that would define certain matters as being those on which the Community and the British Government would agree to consult and exchange information. It might also include certain precise undertakings in the field and would, finally, establish permanent machinery for its implementation. In such a form of external association, it could not be expected that the United Kingdom could have any direct influence on the Community's own development.

The Treaty setting up the Coal and Steel Community came into force on August 10, 1952, when the High Authority met for the first time. The Community's institutions were established at Luxembourg and the British Government set up a delegation to it on September 1st. It became clear that the attitude of the French and German Governments precluded the idea of Britain being permitted to enter the Community under a scheme of partial membership. A powerful interdepartmental committee with Cabinet Office chairmanship and including representatives of the Treasury, the Ministry of Supply, the Board of Trade, the Ministry of Fuel and Power and the Foreign Office, came to the conclusion that Britain should seek some form of external association, and in the spring of 1953 a working party, under Treasury chairmanship, was set up to decide the form that such association should take.

This working party reported in July 1953, when it recommended for steel the establishment of a Common Market between the United Kingdom and Coal and Steel Community, and common action to deal with shortages and surpluses both within the Market and with reference to countries outside it. It was further proposed that there should be regular consultation between the British Government and the Community, which should include the matter of Britain's other commitments. There was to be co-operation in research, no discrimination on transport charges and no restrictions on the movement of labour.

The steel industry was consulted about this plan. By now, of course, there was a difference in the situation in that steel had been denationalized. There was henceforth, therefore, a difference in regard to the character of consultation as between coal and steel. The Coal Board could speak both as a Government agency and as an employer, whereas the Steel Board had to take into account the separate concern of the individual steel companies. The very tight form of association for steel proposed in 1953 was not attractive to the industry, which thought that it unduly restricted its freedom, nor to the Board of Trade, which was worried as to whether the scheme would be acceptable to GATT and again brought up the possible repercussions in the Commonwealth. The scheme was also unfavourably regarded by the British delegation to OEEC and since by this time the British Government was very concerned again to maintain the prestige and influence of OEEC as the main instrument of British economic policy in Europe, this objection carried considerable weight.

The delegation at Luxembourg was instructed to negotiate for a form of association, but the original proposals of the working party were much diluted. The resulting agreement was signed on December 21, 1954 (Cmd. 9346) and was submitted to the House of Commons on February 21, 1955, when it received general approval; it went into effect on September 20, 1955.[1]

The agreement set up a standing Council of Association, composed of four representatives of the Authority and four of the United Kingdom. Provision was also made for British representation at meetings of the Council of Ministers of the Community when they were dealing with matters of joint concern to the Community and the United Kingdom. It was provided that the Council of Association should be the instrument for a continuous exchange of information, and for consultation in regard to matters of common interest concerning coal and steel and, where appropriate, for the co-ordination of action. There were to be consultations before any of the partners introduced new restrictions on trade in coal or steel, if possible before such restrictions were introduced, and for considering co-ordinated action in the event of a decline, either in the demand for these commodities or in their supply. There should be an examination of all forms of restriction upon the flow of trade in coal and steel between the United Kingdom and the Community, with a view to formulating proposals for their reduction or elimination.

In other words, what was done now was to accept the existence of the Coal and Steel Community as a single operating authority for these industries within the six countries, and to establish regular machinery for arriving, through bilateral agreement, at such arrangements as seemed most advantageous to the two sides. It was an application, one might say, of the OEEC formula to a restricted field.

Historians of the British coal and steel industries in the period after 1954 will not be required to pay much attention to the Council of Association. The reasons why the British and the continental industries did not come closer together were not all on the British side. Different economic interests within the Coal and Steel Community did not all see the problem in the same light. Some were thinking entirely in terms of the advantages to be gained from a wider market, while others were more concerned with the long-term political effects. It was possibly because of these differences that on June 21, 1956, the Assembly of the Coal and Steel Community resolved that the activities of the Council of Association should, in future, be supervised by a joint

[1] E. Haas, *The Uniting of Europe* (London, 1958), pp. 99 ff.

parliamentary commission consisting of nine British members of Parliament and nine members of the Common Assembly; but this resolution was never carried into effect.

As has been seen, the question of the relations between the British coal and steel industries and those on the continent was first posed in terms of a shortage of these commodities. With a change in this situation, where coal was concerned, the Council of Association appeared to take on a new importance. Early in 1959 Germany imposed certain quota limitations on imports of coal from outside the Community which were alleged to favour the Americans at the expense of the British. The Council of Association provided a useful forum for arguing against this alleged discrimination, though there were, of course, those who said that Britain would have been in a still stronger position, from the point of view of safeguarding her own interests, had she been a full member of the Community.

The developments in international economic organization in the period after 1954 were accounted for by new but divergent trends of thought within Britain on the one hand, and the 'Little Six' on the other. In Britain, after the disappointment of certain hopes in 1952-3 that a new world-wide system of trade and payments might after all be set up, there was a renewed determination to make the best of OEEC from the point of view of bringing about the widest possible liberalization of trade and payments in Europe. On the other hand, the 'Little Six' were primarily concerned to renew the drive towards greater economic integration with the accent upon the political advantages to be derived therefrom. The first thinking along these lines coincided with the negotiations for the European Defence Community. The so-called Beyen Plan, which was examined by the 'Little Six' in 1953-4, would have set up a common market and customs union. Since this was directly connected with the proposed defence community, it was natural that Britain should be omitted from consideration.[1]

The so-called 'relance Européenne' began with the Messina Conference of the foreign ministers of the 'Little Six' in May

[1] An account of subsequent developments from the point of view of a Belgian negotiator will be found in the article 'Les Etapes de la Co-operation Européenne et les négotiations relatives à une zone libre échange' by Baron Snoy et d'Oppuers in *Chronique de Politique Etrangère* (Brussels), Vol. XII, No. 5-6, September-November 1959.

1955. The ministers, who had met to choose a successor to Jean Monnet as the head of the High Authority of the Coal and Steel Community, were confronted with a set of Benelux proposals based upon the Beyen Plan. The ministers agreed in principle to study the integration of transport, electric power and nuclear energy and also the possibility of setting up a general common market. A group of experts, under the general leadership of M. Spaak, met in Brussels to look into these questions over the period July–December 1955. As a member of the recently created Western European Union, the British Government was invited to take part in these talks and was represented by a delegation with observer status led by an under-secretary from the Board of Trade. There were British members in each of the expert groups.

In December, M. Spaak decided that enough preparatory work had been done and that it was now the time for political decisions. The British were now again confronted, as in 1950, with the question of whether they wished to commit themselves in principle to the proposed objectives before going further, and in the light of their unwillingness to do so, the British participation in the talks came to an end. It has been suggested that the principal reason was that the Six were clearly moving in the direction of a common market, that is to say a group of countries with free trade between themselves and a common external tariff and away from the idea preferred by the British of a free trade area which would have left the participating countries free to maintain their own external tariffs. Commonwealth preferences and other overseas requirements, possibly including a desire to be unhampered in commercial negotiations with the United States, were taken as the reason for the British insistence on this point which was to be so marked over the next few years.

Spaak's report in April to the ministers of the Six, did not raise the question of British participation and emphasized the political aspects of the new proposals. The basic decisions by the Six were taken at the Venice meeting on May 29–30, 1956. The principle decision was that the Six should go ahead and conclude their own treaties, but leave the door open for other countries either to adhere to the treaties or to propose some form of association with the new Community. In résponse to this, on July 19, 1956, the Council of OEEC decided to study the possibility of a multilateral association between the Six and the remaining member countries of OEEC.

The treaties between the Six were signed at Rome on March 25, 1957. They established the European Economic Community or Common Market and the European Atomic Energy Community, Euratom. Both treaties came into force on January 1, 1958, and the first meeting of the European Parliamentary Assembly, which incorporated the Common Assembly of the European Coal and Steel Community as well as supplying an assembly for the Common Market and Euratom, opened on March 19, 1958. The Treaties of Rome were generally held to mark a retreat from the full principle of supranationalism as conceived by the makers of the Coal and Steel Community. In the Common Market, the Commission was less important than the Council of Ministers, though the latter, since it acted by weighted majority voting, or could do so, and did not have to be unanimous, also embodied the idea of a Community.

The subsequent development of the machinery of the Common Market was to carry its mode of action some distance from that envisaged in the Treaty. Under the Treaty it had been for the Commission to make proposals and for the Council of Ministers to ratify them. Actually there was a close interlocking of the work of the Secretariat of the Commission with the national governments, and again of the Secretariat of the Council of Ministers with those governments, so that a very general consensus was arrived at, largely through informal means, before the members of the Council of Ministers at their monthly meetings were faced with the need to make binding decisions.

The atomic energy side can be dealt with fairly briefly as far as the British attitude is concerned. The European Atomic Commission was set up as a five member executive to carry out policy and make proposals, with considerable autonomy in research, the procurement of ores and the inspection of industrial establishments in relation to its security code. The restrictions upon the Commission's own independent powers made the right of the European Parliamentary Assembly to unseat it, by a motion of censure, of little importance. But the Assembly was given an important role in relation to the research and investment budgets of Euratom and had the right to be consulted in other respects. The British found this structure unacceptable, partly because of the surviving elements of supranationalism, and partly because of the feeling that Britain could better exploit its then considerable lead in atomic technology if it remained in a more independent position. This, at least, was the view of the British Atomic Energy Commission, even though it was not fully shared by the industrial interests concerned.

In this field one must again emphasize the special relationship between Britain and the United States arising from the military significance of developments in the atomic field. It was felt that if Britain went into any system involving the sharing of information on atomic questions, this would adversely affect her ties with the United States. In fact, until the revision of the MacMahon Act in 1958, the amount of information made available to Britain by the United States was very limited.

Britain was not unwilling to see some measure of co-operation in the field of nuclear energy on a less intensive basis, and in June 1955, the Council of Ministers of OEEC had set up a commission for nuclear energy under which a working party looked into this problem.

In February 1956, the Council of Ministers of OEEC discussed the possible relations between the proposed work of this organization in the atomic field and that of Euratom. The British participants in this discussion, the Foreign Secretary and the Chancellor of the Exchequer, voiced their belief in the importance of co-operation on the wider basis made possible by OEEC.

In July 1956, the Council approved the report of a special committee on nuclear energy set up at the February meeting, and proceeded to set up a Steering Committee for Nuclear Energy, which included the members and associate members of OEEC. It was agreed that any group of members could set up working groups in this field without involving all the others. Various such groups were set up, the United Kingdom co-operating in one of these with the Scandinavian countries, Austria, Portugal, Switzerland and Turkey. A group was also set up to maintain liaison with Euratom. The Council instructed the Steering Committee to draft a statute for security controls and to arrange for an agreement between the OEEC and the International Atomic Energy Agency. In December 1957, an OEEC Security Convention was signed which was intended to prevent jointly developed nuclear facilities from being used for military purposes.

On December 20th a statute was signed setting up the European Nuclear Energy Agency for co-ordinating research and development. This body came into existence on February 1, 1958. A year later, on February 4, 1959, the United Kingdom signed an agreement of its own with Euratom for the exchange of information and materials. And on March 23, 1959, an agreement was signed for co-operation between the United Kingdom, Euratom and the European Nuclear Energy Agency for co-operation on the Winfrith Heath project. By this time it looked as though the European countries might progress faster than had originally been thought likely, and that the British self-exclusion from Euratom might prove to be an error as putting her in a weaker position as far as her exports in this industry were concerned.

All this was, however, by now a rather speculative question, in view of the changing climate of opinion about the future energy problems of Europe and the likely role of nuclear energy in the coming years. Opinion was also affected by the more far reaching debate over inter-European trade generally, precipitated by the advent and development of the Common Market.

Britain's reasons for being unwilling to take part in the proposed Common Market at the end of 1955 have already been indicated. But industry was naturally concerned about the possibility that a successful termination of the Common Market negotiations would leave it in an unfavourable competitive position. Consultations were therefore held concerning the likely effects of a wider association, which would embody the principle of free trade between its members, but leave their autonomy in external tariffs unaffected. At the July 1956 meeting of the Council of Ministers of OEEC, the Chancellor of the Exchequer, Mr Macmillan, declared that while Britain would not join the Common Market, she would welcome the formation of a free trade area including all the OEEC countries, but limited to industrial products. A working party of OEEC was set up to consider the feasibility of this association and the project was commended for its political significance by the Prime Minister, Sir Anthony Eden, at the Llandudno Conference of the Conservative Party in October.

During this winter the negotiations between the Six went ahead with considerable speed. On the other hand, nothing was done for some time about the proposals for a free trade area because Mr Macmillan had promised M. Spaak to leave the matter in abeyance lest it should impede the negotiations of the Common Market Treaty itself. But the House of Commons was informed on November 26th that talks about a free trade area were in progress. The Opposition in Parliament showed itself favourable, as did the Trades Union Congress. The Federation of British Industries, as might be expected, was somewhat divided since clearly different industries would be differently affected.

Ministerial opinion was probably mixed also. As we have seen the actual machinery on the official side was not new, but the scale of it increased considerably once the free trade area idea was launched. There was now an operation on a scale similar to that of 1947, and perhaps covering an even greater breadth of subject matter. Between the launching of the idea and the suspension of negotiations in November 1958, eight departments of government were heavily and continuously concerned; namely, the Treasury, the Foreign Office, the Board of Trade, the Commonwealth, Relations Office, the Colonial Office, the Ministry of Agriculture, Fisheries and Food, the Ministry of Power and the Board of Customs and Excise. Several other departments were concerned, though to a lesser extent.

The work in Whitehall was of a different kind, however, to that of the Marshall Plan period when it was a matter of dealing with rather precise quantities. What was now required was speculative thought on future relations in Europe as regards both trade and general economic and political development. Precise quantitative answers were demanded as to the likely effect of particular proposals, and these could not always be supplied. Although there was little parliamentary discussion in this period to distract the attention of the negotiators, an unusual number of government publications were issued illustrating the progress of the idea. It was held by those concerned that these indicated a genuine willingness to experiment and that the stumbling blocks, which ultimately proved fatal, did not arise from differences over mere machinery.

M. Spaak came to London for talks with the British ministers in January 1957. He then explained the state of negotiations for a Common Market which by now British opinion took as likely to come into being despite some earlier scepticism based upon the experience of the proposed European Defence Community. In the course of his discussions with Mr Thorneycroft, who had succeeded Mr Macmillan at the Treasury when the latter became Prime Minister on the resignation of Sir Anthony Eden, and with the President of the Board of Trade, Sir David Eccles, M. Spaak undertook that the Treaty would include a specific article permitting either the bilateral or multilateral association of other European countries with it.

In February 1957, the Council of Ministers of OEEC, under Mr Thorneycroft's chairmanship, agreed in principle to the setting up of a free trade area and created three working parties, who were given the tasks of drafting a convention on free trade in industrial products, discussing the expansion of trade in agricultural products and looking into the special problems of the underdeveloped countries within the OEEC area. Under pressure from M. Spaak, who had illustrated the advantages of political leadership in negotiations of this kind, Mr Thorneycroft agreed to take personal charge of co-ordinating these activities. It was agreed that he should report back to the Council about them by the end of July, but since the ratification of the Rome Treaties was incomplete at that date the matter was, in fact, left over until October. This was done with the clear understanding, on the British side, that these negotiations would be resumed immediately ratification was complete.[1]

The British proposals for a free trade area had been made public in February. It was to be narrowly constituted in that it would be limited to removing tariffs on industrial products and would involve the participating countries in as few consequential obligations as possible. This was quite different in idea from the European Economic Community which included elaborate arrangements for the harmonization of economic and social conditions. For this reason the institutions required for the proposed free trade area need not, in the British view, be of the elaborate kind envisaged in the Common Market Treaty. They were outlined indeed in a single paragraph of the British proposals:

'HMG recognize that, as the Working Party have pointed out, the precise nature of the institutions of the FTA cannot be

---

[1] See the statement by Mr Reginald Maudling in the House of Commons on November 11, 1958.

determined in advance of the definition of the form and substance of the Area itself. In the view of HMG the FTA should be established within OEEC. Some departure from the unanimity rule will be necessary in certain carefully defined matters, for example where a country seeks a release from one of the original obligations and with remedying any failure to do so. It is clear that there should be close co-ordination between the institutions of the FTA and those of the Customs and Economic Union, so as to simplify administration and to facilitate the observance of their dual obligations by those countries which are members of both organizations' (Cmnd. 72, 1957, par. 24).

It is clear that from 1957 onwards there was a very considerable degree of commitment in British Government circles to the idea of a free trade area, and a belief that one would eventually be negotiated along the lines suggested in the British memorandum. It also seems likely that public opinion and industrial opinion in Britain moved in a direction favourable to the project. This is as true, it seems, of the Opposition as of the Government. For this reason there was little discussion in Parliament, but the Labour Party maintained its own contacts with OEEC Secretariat and was thus well briefed on the subject.

Expert opinion noted that in addition to the direct repercussions of a free trade area upon British trade and industry, there was a financial aspect in that it would have meant an increased risk of short-term crisis in the balance of payments; but British policy was unaffected by this consideration. It may be noted, in passing, that there was a movement on foot to change the existing system of intra-European payments. When the Council of OEEC discussed the EPU in June 1955, the British representative argued that once sterling and other European currencies had been made fully convertible, the need for a multilateral clearing system would disappear. This was not accepted by all countries, but it was agreed that arrangements should be made to replace the EPU by a new European monetary agreement to take effect when a proportion of countries had gone over to convertibility. Under such a system the Board of Management of the EMA would set up a European fund for providing short-term credit to countries which might get into difficulties with their balance of payments. The multilateral clearing system would be used for settling balances at regular intervals at known rates of exchange. This agreement, in fact, came into force on December 27, 1958.

When the Rome Treaty was published, important new problems were revealed. The question had arisen as to whether overseas territories of the members of the Common Market should, or should not, be included in the new arrangements. At one stage, indeed, the British had been told by the French that overseas territories would not come in. The British asked that before a decision was reached they and the Portuguese should be consulted, but were told that this would be very difficult. Eventually a meeting did take place between British officials and representatives of the Six in Paris on February 15, 1957. At this meeting M. Spaak said that the whole question was still undecided and that the British objections made it more difficult to reach a decision. Nevertheless, it was announced by the Six on February 20, that the overseas territories would be included. And it is believed that a decision to this effect was reached only one or two days after the talks with the British. It was a political decision, taken at the highest level, as part of the price paid for French acceptance of the scheme.

The British Government, although taken by surprise at this juncture, had, of course, been keeping under review the relations between the colonial territories and Commonwealth countries and the proposed Common Market. There had been only one formal meeting with representatives of colonial governments (in March 1957) but there was a constant flow of information to and consultation with the governments in the colonial territories themselves. As we have seen, the Colonial Office, like the Commonwealth Relations Office, was represented throughout the period on the main interdepartmental committee.

With regard to the independent members of the Commonwealth, the British memorandum of February 1957 had pointed out that the British association with the Common Market would be limited by our obligations to them. This question was also kept in review throughout the subsequent negotiations. Mr John Edwards, who was one of the Labour members who had followed the negotiations in detail, pointed out in the House of Commons on February 12, 1959, that the British Blue Book on the negotiations (Cmnd. 641, 1959) did not give any real indication as to the importance attached to this aspect of the question.

The Commonwealth countries most directly interested were, on the one hand, Canada, because of possible balance of payments questions, and on the other, Australia and New Zealand, anxious about their own trade with the United Kingdom. It has been argued that the Commonwealth countries themselves might have been able to come to an arrangement for a system of mutual preferences with the countries of the Common Market, though here a difficulty would be presented by the existence of GATT. It was even reported that the German and Italian Governments had given certain Commonwealth countries assurances along these lines. The belief that Commonwealth obligations were no insurmountable obstacle to free trade area proposals is supported by an agreement reached at the unofficial Commonwealth Conference, in New Zealand held in January 1959. This Conference, which included Cabinet Ministers from Australia and New Zealand and members of the legislatures of South Africa, India, Southern Rhodesia, Ceylon and Malaya, as well as British parliamentarians and also economists from all the older Commonwealth countries, unanimously agreed 'that a new approach was needed in the negotiations with the Six countries of Europe . . . that the Government of the United Kingdom and the other Commonwealth countries should urgently consider the advisability of conducting joint negotiations . . . that the Commonwealth should be prepared to consider variations in the system of mutual preferences . . . that such associations would entail some degree of sacrifice on the part of all Commonwealth countries . . . that the free entry of staple foodstuffs into the United Kingdom should be preserved . . . and that the United States of America should be invited to assist in securing a satisfactory solution'.

It has, however, been pointed out, that if it had actually come down to bargaining between the Commonwealth and the Common Market, the situation would have arisen in which countries like Australia and New Zealand would be trying to get their agricultural goods into Europe, while the Europeans wished to protect their home agriculture and get their manufactures into Australia and New Zealand, who were, themselves, anxious to protect their own industry. Once again, the attitudes of all the six Common Market countries were probably not identical on this issue.

There was also a theoretical difficulty in the idea of a special relationship between the Common Market countries and the independent members of the Commonwealth. It was difficult to see why exceptions should be made for independent countries in other continents just because they happened to be members of the Commonwealth. If India were taken into the system as well as Australia, it looked like becoming a world-wide arrangement rather than a European one. If some countries in the Commonwealth were included and others were left out, then this would have been a factor of division in the Commonwealth itself. As far as the dependent territories were concerned it was the more difficult to devise appropriate proposals in view of the rapidity with which many of them were graduating towards independence in this period. It was generally felt that if the outcome of the talks was to be an industrial free trade area, British colonies should not be included with the exception of Hongkong and possibly Kenya.

A different problem was that raised by the creation of a Development Fund in the Treaty of Rome the need for which had not been established in the British view.

Germany and France ratified the Rome Treaties in July, Italy in October, Luxembourg and Belgium in November, and the Netherlands in December. The British, meanwhile, had been holding some partial consultations. The proposed free trade area was discussed at a meeting of the body that dealt with Anglo-Scandinavian trade relations, Uniscan, in June 1957, and in the same month, it was agreed, in bilateral talks with the Dutch, that a free trade area would be an essential complement to the Common Market. Once the French and German ratifications were through it was possible to take up the free trade area negotiations once more.

On August 7th, it was announced from No. 10 Downing Street that Mr Maudling was to supervise and co-ordinate the Government's preparations for the forthcoming discussions and would act as their representative in them. The announcement continued 'the Paymaster General will work in consultation with the ministers departmentally concerned with these matters, in particular the Foreign Secretary, the Chancellor of the Exchequer (who also has special responsibilities in this connection as chairman of the OEEC) and the President of the Board of Trade. The Paymaster General will report to the Prime Minister. He will continue to discharge his present functions, but for these additional duties he will have a special office in Gwydyr House together with a small staff.'

At a meeting in October of the Council of Ministers of OEEC Mr Thorneycroft announced that his other responsibilities made it impossible for him to give sufficient time to the co-ordination of the free trade area negotiations. On October 17th, therefore, a Steering Committee for the negotiations was set up with Mr Maudling as chairman. Mr Thorneycroft, as chairman of the Council of Ministers, was still to be the principal co-ordinator, but the actual task of negotiating between the different Governments was to be undertaken by Mr Maudling with a Foreign Office official at the head of his staff. At the London end of the negotiations there was now established a special committee which met weekly until the breakdown of the talks in November 1958. This committee dealt with all the departments concerned as well as the Commonwealth aspect and became the principal focus of activity. It was, as usual, under non-departmental Treasury chairmanship.

The use of a minister for negotiations of this kind was a departure for Britain, although other countries have used ministers, or even set up special ministries for handling international economic problems of this kind. It has been suggested that one reason for the British decision was the hope of persuading other countries to use ministers also, so as to speed decisions. On the British side the use of an individual minister, able to go backwards and forwards between Paris and London and to keep in direct touch with the whole range of problems involved, did diminish the need for elaborate paper work. On the other hand, it should not be forgotten that the minister's position was that of a negotiator only. He still had to refer to his Government for any important decisions. Otherwise departmental responsibilities in the field would have been thoroughly blurred. Mr Maudling's colleagues in the Economic Policy Committee of the Cabinet discussed with him, as occasion arose, the general line that he was to take in relation to the various stages of the negotiations. As these negotiations were ultimately unsuccessful, attention has been directed to this new departure. It has been argued that a negotiator at the official level would have been just as effective and that, by using a minister, we committed too much of the prestige of the Government to what proved a doubtful enterprise. Quite apart from the contention made in some quarters that no negotiation should be entrusted to anyone not professionally trained for the task, there is the point that a minister may find it more difficult to go back on something he has said than an official who could more easily plead new instructions. Finally, it was later argued that even if it was right to give Mr Maudling the task of acting as the British negotiator, he should have declined chairmanship of the Intergovernmental Steering Committee since this weakened his position as an advocate of the British point of view.

It is, of course, impossible to come to any definite conclusions on a matter of this kind. Some foreign observers of these events took the view that a more important factor in the ultimate failure had been Mr Thorneycroft's resignation as Chancellor of the Exchequer on January 6, 1958, since they believed that this removed from the British team the minister most alive to the continental point of view. If it is true, as has been said, that the British conducted the negotiations as though the difficulties to be overcome were exclusively of an economic and technical kind, whereas in reality the core of the argument was political, then this goes back to the original underestimation at the time of the Messina Conference of the drive behind the 'relance Européenne', and this underestimation was shared even by some of the Messina statesmen themselves—they were surprised at their own success.

It is only necessary to summarize very briefly the subsequent course of the negotiations. Various intergovernmental meetings were held towards the end of 1957, and in January 1958, Britain put forward a memorandum on the agricultural aspects of the problem. In February there were visits by Mr Maudling to three of the other OEEC countries outside the Six, namely Sweden, Switzerland and Austria. A French memorandum indicated that the French now had strong objections to the original free trade area proposals and that in return for any concession to Britain, they would want to call into question the maintenance of Commonwealth preferences and would require access to Britain's colonial territories. Italy and Germany attempted to produce compromise proposals, but after the change of the regime in France in May the whole question was clearly one of the line that would be taken by General de Gaulle's administration, and bilateral talks were held with the French in June and July. By now the British negotiators were pessimistic but the Scandinavians did not wish the effort to come to an agreement to be abandoned.

In July a new set of French proposals were made at a meeting of the Steering Committee under Mr Maudling's chairmanship. The six countries held a meeting at Venice in September when hopes were still held out that a free trade area would be agreed to, but strong French objections were indicated to the British Government early in November, and on November 14th, a French ministerial statement announced that France would not accept any formal association which did not include a provision for a single tariff between the six participants and the rest of the world. Attempts were made by the Germans and the Benelux countries to find a compromise. On December 15th there was a major dispute at an OEEC ministerial meeting when the non-Common Market countries including Britain, whose spokesman was the President of the Board of Trade, talked about possible reprisals should the Common Market powers not change their attitude about new quota arrangements due to come into force at the beginning of the new year. The open breach was patched up and new proposals were made by the British which were turned down at a meeting of the ministers of the Six on January 14, 1959. Thereafter the negotiations for a free trade area petered out, though as late as April 27th, Mr Maudling, speaking in the Council of Europe, indicated that the British Government was still hopeful for some arrangement. By May 1959, Britain's energies had been turned towards the task of creating a free trade association with other members of OEEC who were not in the Common Market. Talks on these lines proceeded during the summer and autumn and a treaty creating the so-called 'Outer Seven' with the Scandinavian countries, Switzerland, Austria and Portugal was initialled at Stockholm on November 20, 1959.

The breakdown of the negotiations for the free trade area was something of a shock to the British Government who, as Mr Maudling told the House of Commons on February 12, 1959, had been assured as late as the previous October of the determination of the Six to seek an association on a multilateral basis with the other members of OEEC. It had clearly been expected in London that the commercial advantages of the proposed free trade area to certain countries in the Six, notably Germany, would outweigh the protectionism of France. In other words, there seems to have been a wrong assessment of the extent to which Germany was prepared to exercise pressure upon France and this, in turn, may have arisen from a wrong estimate of the balance of political forces in Germany itself. It is known that the German Chancellor and Foreign Minister were in agreement in the importance they attached to the long-range political implications of the Common Market and Euratom, while the Minister for Economics, Herr Erhard, thought of these institutions as protectionist and dirigistic and was in favour of the wider association. What was perhaps insufficiently appreciated was that Erhard's record showed that when his ideas conflicted with those of the Chancellor it was the latter who invariably came out on top. The British may also have been involuntarily misled by some of their German informants. In the German foreign service itself there could be found individuals who would give an impression favourable to the chances of the free trade area. Critics of the British handling of the matter have suggested the possibility that the French position was also wrongly assessed and that some official circles in London may have given too little weight to the reports of French political opposition to the scheme that reached them through diplomatic channels. The Treasury officials who came to Paris on OEEC business at this period, may not have known the senior French officials well enough to appreciate the full strength of their convictions on this subject. These suggestions may fortify a view that has been expressed to the effect that Britain should not have accepted the chairmanship of the OEEC Council of Ministers back in 1952, or should have given it up before the free trade area negotiations began. It has been argued that this position implied a commitment to particular forms of negotiation, while others might with advantage have been explored.

To these points, some of which were made by Opposition spokesmen in the House of Commons debate on February 12, 1959, it may perhaps be added that the British handling of their idea was occasionally clumsy. For instance, it has been suggested that the proposed name for the new organization was unnecessarily uninspiring. As early as October 1957, a competent private observer of the European economic scene wrote 'the title European Economic Community has a corporate and constructive

sound. By contrast, free trade area is an uninspiring term, suggesting little more than a gaggle of customs officials'.

Nevertheless, too much should not be made of the breakdown
of the free trade area negotiations in considering the effectiveness or otherwise of British machinery. Ultimately, it all came
down to individual decisions of such highly incalculable personalities as Adenauer and de Gaulle. The French had kept holding
out hopes that they would agree in the end and that their series
of counter-proposals to our own were seriously meant, while
other countries kept appealing to us for patience. It was only just
before the Venice Conference in September 1958 that the French
apparently persuaded the Germans to accept their point of view
and to make a complete *volte face* on the question of the nature of
the free trade area.

Should the real cause of the breakdown then be sought in the
British objections to supranationalism? In this connection it is
interesting to note that developments within the Coal and Steel
Community in the course of 1959 seem to show some relaxation
of its supranational aspects, and a growing preference for direct
governmental action on the part of the three larger member
countries. This was shown in the rejection of the High Authority's proposals for dealing with the coal crisis of that year.

These developments justified, to some extent perhaps, the
original British scepticism about the likelihood of countries
accepting the decisions of a supranational authority when important questions of employment were involved. But, of course,
the crisis in the affairs of the European Coal and Steel Community was also related to the anti-integrationist attitude of the
new French regime. While this regime was prepared to press
on with the successive stages in bringing about the European
Common Market, it made it clear that its fidelity to its undertakings in this respect was the product of economic considerations, and that it did not accept the federalist presuppositions of
the Community's original sponsors. Indeed, by September 1959
the French Government was clearly moving towards the idea of
trying to get its partners to modify the text of the Coal and Steel
Community Treaty so as to align the powers of the High
Authority with the less considerable ones of the Commission in
the European Economic Community.[1]

[1] See the account of the French proposals in *Le Monde*, September 11, 1959.

The differences in approach between Britain and the Six were also apparent in the more general problem of trying to rationalize the family of European and Atlantic institutions which were successively developed in this period. It was undeniable that there was a good deal of overlapping. For instance, defence was the responsibility of NATO and of WEU and was discussed in the WEU Assembly. But the Council of Europe discussed general questions of foreign policy, that is to say, the reasons for defence and the threats against which defence was necessary. On the economic side, the Council of Europe discussed the right of establishment, the relation of welfare systems to the migration of labour, and questions of tourism, while all these things were being handled at the inter-governmental level by the OEEC. The British Government throughout the period was concerned to avoid this excessive proliferation of institutions, partly on the grounds of the desirability of economizing in money and personnel, and partly because it was felt that this proliferation contributed to their generally low standing in the public eye. On the other hand, the countries of the Six, after 1950, tended to take the view that any British suggestions for linking their joint institutions more closely to the wider European or Atlantic ones, were symptoms of a British desire to hinder the further development of Western European integration along federalist lines.

The first proposal of this kind was the so-called Eden Plan put to the Committee of Ministers of the Council of Europe on March 19, 1952. The idea was so to remodel the Council of Europe as to enable its organs, and particularly its Consultative Assembly, to serve the needs also of the Coal and Steel Community and of the proposed European Defence Community. This proposal was not successful, as the Common Assembly of the Coal and Steel Community was, at this time, hoping for the creation of a European political community with institutions of its own, as the counterpart to the proposed European Defence Community.[1] Since these plans too collapsed, what remained of the Eden Plan was the establishment of certain links between the Coal and Steel Community and the Council of Europe: 'They included the transmission of reports to the Council by both the High Authority and the Common Assembly joint sessions of the

[1] See Anthony Nutting, *Europe will not wait* (London, 1960), Chap. VIII.

two Assemblies and joint sessions between the High Authority and Committees of the Council, including the Committee of Ministers.'[1]

The next British effort was made after the passage of the Rome Treaties when there was also the complication of the existence of WEU with a Parliamentary Assembly of its own. This meant by now that continental parliamentarians had to man delegations to three Assemblies and the British to two, not including, in either case, the unofficial NATO Parliamentarians Conference.

This further British initiative was sketched for the first time when the Foreign Secretary, Mr Selwyn Lloyd, took part in a discussion in the NATO Council on the report of the 'Three Wise Men' at its meeting in Paris on December 12, 1956. He then said, according to press reports, that he saw the report of the 'Three Wise Men' against the wider background of an Atlantic Community within which there would function a strong European Community. This was what he called a 'background of a grand design'. The 'grand design' would be built according to a threefold pattern. High political and military direction would be given by NATO, with WEU functioning within its framework. Economic co-operation would be carried out under, and in association with, the OEEC. Finally, there would be an assembly on parliamentary lines, with powers and functions still to be assigned to it, which would complete the institutions of the Atlantic Community. The British idea, declared the Foreign Secretary, was that there had been enough multiplication of institutions and that the need now was for streamlining and simplification.

The formal British proposals were presented to the Council of Europe by the Minister of State for Foreign Affairs, Mr Ormsby-Gore, on May 1, 1957. Aware, no doubt, that Mr Selwyn Lloyd's original version of the grand design had been critically received on the Continent, Mr Ormsby-Gore insisted upon the all-inclusive approach of his Government. He used his speech not only for outlining proposals with regard to the European Assemblies, but also for giving other evidence of Britain's genuine interest in European matters; for instance, her readiness to contribute a share to the development of the peaceful uses of atomic energy.

[1] See Robertson, *European Institutions*, p. 76.

Mr Ormsby-Gore denied that Britain regarded with anything but the utmost goodwill the efforts of the Messina
Powers to put forward the work of integration as between
themselves on the lines they had chosen, but repeated the
familiar reasons why Britain could not join them. Britain's own
policies, he declared, were intended as a contribution to building
up Europe's potential strength so that she might become 'a
stronger partner' within the Atlantic Community. He went over
the whole situation within the Atlantic Alliance and discussed
the reasons for the British advocacy of a free trade area and the
possibility of associating with it the countries of the Commonwealth.

Although Britain was not willing to enter into institutional
arrangements which would take final political and economic
decisions out of her hands, Mr Ormsby-Gore stressed the fact
that the British proposals need not interfere with the plans of
the Six. For instance, Britain's wish to make the OEEC, with
its wide membership, the continuing framework for developing
co-operation, both in the economic field and in respect of nuclear
energy, was not to suggest that it should 'attempt to swallow
up the economic communities of the Six which have a special
and important role to fill'. Again, while emphasizing the fact
that the majority of the countries represented at Strasbourg
were not prepared to 'contemplate giving an international parliament executive power', he went on to say: 'I know that the
Six have already done so and these powers give their Assembly
a quite different character from this Assembly, or the WEU
Assembly or the Conference of NATO Parliamentarians. We all
recognize that the Assembly of the Six has an executive task to
carry out; and except, perhaps, for sharing administrative facilities, and participating in joint sessions, it is not our wish to
encroach upon its activities in any way.'

The aim of the grand design was threefold: 'To bring the
activities of the various European and Atlantic organizations to
the attention of our peoples at home; to expose the inter-
governmental activities within those organizations to constructive parliamentary criticism; and to stimulate member governments of the Western Alliance to be vigilant in its defence, and
in striving to strengthen and improve it.'

The governing idea, as far as machinery was concerned, was

to replace the multiplicity of assemblies with a single one which should have direct relations with all the inter-governmental organizations, that is to say, with NATO and WEU, the OEEC, the European Conference of Ministers of Transport and so on. This made it clear that the institutions of the Six would not be involved, but even so there were difficulties in that the membership of the main inter-governmental organizations was not identical in each case. This problem would be met by dividing up the work of the single assembly between different commissions:

'We visualize there being one such commission for economic affairs, one for political affairs, one for social and cultural affairs, one for legal and administrative affairs. Not all the participating countries would wish to be represented on all of these Commissions. Each commission would, in fact, be semi-autonomous. Some of you, for example, would not wish to take part on the Defence Commission. But for the convenience of yourselves and of Ministers when they attend, and in the interests of efficiency and economy, the Commissions would all meet in one place and be served by a single Secretariat—with perhaps the Defence Secretariat set apart. And in general the wider the attendance the better. We would, for instance, hope that the "neutral" European countries would all participate as fully as possible from the outset. The Americans and Canadians, who are of course our Atlantic allies, might also participate where appropriate. If we build the relations between these Assembly Commissions and the various inter-governmental organizations on the basis of perhaps an obligation on the part of those organizations to provide an annual report but otherwise on *ad hoc* arrangements—such as joint committees and so on—we think they would not only work better than some of our present arrangements but it would also make it easier for those countries which find themselves in a special position to participate.'

It was emphasized that this was not a cut-and-dried plan but subject to negotiation between governments as well as to discussion in the Consultative Assembly. But the general line of British thinking was fairly obvious. To use what became the standing image, the new assembly would be like a chest-of-drawers with five drawers any one of which could be pulled out as the occasion dictated. Each country could choose whether to be present when any particular drawer was pulled out, or whether to absent itself. In other words, a country which, by reason of its proximity to the Soviet Union or because of its neutrality, felt that it could, for example, only participate in the discussion of social questions or cultural matters, could avoid being concerned with more dangerous topics.

The debate in the House of Commons on February 8, 1957, that is to say a few months earlier, had shown that proposals of this kind commanded widespread support in Britain, not least among those Members of Parliament who had had experience of the European Assemblies. There was also evident some desire for a British lead. Nevertheless, the criticism which the scheme received internationally showed that a lead along those lines would carry insufficient conviction. The reasons for this have already been analysed. The whole idea was allowed to fall into the background, while the more immediate question of the Common Market and free trade area occupied the centre of the stage.

The most important of the suggestions inherent in the grand design was that there should be a formal amalgamation of the OEEC and the Council of Europe, two bodies which had already been in close contact for a considerable time. The possibility of such an amalgamation was present in the very early stages of the Council of Europe and referred to in a debate in the House of Commons as early as June 27, 1950. It seems probable that in the early years, the differences in membership, which were alleged as a reason against proceeding with this suggestion, concealed a belief on the part of the OEEC Secretariat that the existence of a parliamentary assembly to which it had to report would be an obstacle to pursuing its proper tasks. But later on the Secretariat came to realize, it is believed, that it might be easier to elicit the necessary popular support for its work if it were given a political sounding-board. There has been a considerable degree of British sympathy for this idea though there is a difficulty in the British conception of the necessary separation between civil servants on the one hand and parliamentarians on the other. This arose when the Council of Europe asked to be allowed to have representatives on the OEEC committees which, from the British point of view, meant an obliteration of this important distinction. Nevertheless, the possibilities of the proposed amalgamation were seriously explored, particularly on the side of the Council of Europe. But from 1957 onwards this idea also was subordinated to the free trade area negotiations on the grounds that, until this matter was cleared up, it would not be possible to know what would be the future shape or prospects of the OEEC itself.

The 'Group of Four' set up in 1960 to consider the future of OEEC, including the steps necessary to bring in the USA and Canada as full members, expressed sympathy with a proposal put forward by the Consultative Assembly of the Council of Europe under which the latter would organize an annual *ad hoc* meeting of parliamentarians from all the countries taking part in the remodelled organization, which would discuss its affairs on the Council of Europe pattern.[1]

[1] *A Remodelled Economic Organization*, 'A Report by the Group of Four' (Paris OEEC, April 1960), p. 54.

116

CHAPTER 5

The Foreign Office and British Representation Abroad

THE preceding chapters have given an outline of Britain's relations with the new international institutions of the period. It must be remembered that this account is far from being adequate to cover the whole of the burden that fell upon the British machinery for conducting external relations. A great deal of the time and energy of the Government was spent on conducting relations arising out of the 'cold war' and out of related crises in the Far East and Middle East. Public opinion all the time, and Government opinion for most of the time, was necessarily far more alive to issues of this kind with the immense dangers they implied. The division which is convenient for the purpose of analysis cannot be applied to the responsible ministers or to the principal officials who served them. And, of course, the major events in world politics helped to produce the climate of opinion in which decisions in our more limited field were made. Finally, these were important years in the testing of the institutions of the United Nations and it was only the failures of these universalist bodies that made for concentration upon the more limited objectives of greater co-operation or co-ordination in the European and Atlantic worlds.

With this warning in mind, we can proceed to examine in rather greater detail the principal agencies through which the British Government worked in relation to the European and Atlantic institutions whose birth and growth we have briefly chronicled. In the present chapter we shall be dealing first with the machinery of the Foreign Office itself, and then with the arrangements for which it was, technically at least, responsible for seeing that the British position was adequately represented at the various institutions. In the next chapter we shall deal with the way in which the other major Whitehall departments with responsibilities in the field of foreign affairs, organized themselves for this part of their duties; and in the succeeding one we shall return to the machinery of inter-departmental co-ordination to which repeated reference has already, necessarily, been made.

We must, however, emphasize that in the view of many of those responsible for working this machinery such a division, while convenient and indeed essential for the purposes of the student, may help to obliterate the reality of the situation. The emphasis, it is held, should now be upon the working of the machinery of government as a whole in the field of external relations, with each department playing the particular role assigned to it by the nature of the immediate task. In this sense, the problem of whether the Foreign Office should be primarily an instrument for negotiation or a department responsible for conducting the nation's affairs in all branches of external relations, economic and cultural as well as political—an argument which confronts us in the case of certain other countries—has no real relevance to the British position in the period with which we are concerned.

It is pointed out that inter-departmental co-operation was thrust upon Whitehall by the demands of the two world wars. It largely disappeared after the first of these, as we have seen, but after the Second World War the habits of co-operation survived, largely because of the great deal of economic work that still remained to be done. This meant a permanent departure from the more formal methods of conducting relations between the Foreign Office and other departments, and the development of many contacts through semi-official correspondence at all levels. Which department would take the lead in framing or executing policy in any particular sphere, would be partly a matter of convenience and partly a question of the relative weight of the ministerial or official personalities involved. Sometimes the issue would be settled by mere geography. Thus, while it was relatively easy for the economic departments to supply the necessary experts for work in Europe, the economic work of SEATO was performed directly by the Foreign Office because of the distance from London of the organization's headquarters.

It is, of course, still legitimate to ask whether there is not, at any rate in certain fields, a specifically Foreign Office point of view. To this question rather different answers will be given by different people. It has been suggested that such differences as exist are likely to be procedural in nature rather than substantive. The Foreign Office has been traditionally geared to using embassies abroad as the channels for contact with other countries and has, therefore, had a problem of adaptation to the new international institutions with their techniques of permanent diplomacy by conference, through large national delegations, representing a variety of competencies. On a more philosophical plane, it is suggested that the Foreign Office necessarily takes a more long-term view of problems than domestic departments, and is prone to thinking in words rather than figures. It is accustomed to permanent problems rather than to questions capable of finite solutions. In particular, it is argued, the strong priority it gave in the period to Anglo-American relations reflects the Foreign Office's concern with the facts of power, to which, however, the answer might be given that for a rather different set of reasons the Treasury, on the whole, also tended to keep the Anglo-American relationship in the foreground.

All discussions of this kind are necessarily highly speculative. What cannot be denied is the enormous growth in the amount of actual day-to-day work falling upon the Foreign Office itself.[1] This could even be demonstrated statistically both in terms of the numbers of persons employed and in terms of the circulation of documents. For instance, the number of incoming dispatches and other papers rose from 68,119 in 1913 to 270,968 in 1939 and to 603,870 in 1949. This figure, which is about nine times that of the pre-First World War period, has since then remained fairly constant, rising to 627,676 in 1951—the peak year—but falling off to 588,949 in 1958. Unfortunately, the breakdown of these figures between the different departments of the Foreign Office cannot conveniently be used to illustrate their relative importance, since some departments of no great political significance—conference and supply, for instance, or

---

[1] See for an official assessment of the reasons for this, the memorandum from the Foreign Office reproduced in the *Seventh Report from the Select Committee on Estimates* Session 1953–4, pp. 17 ff.

passport control—are great producers of documentation. On the other hand, the figures do show the very considerable importance of the departments dealing with economic relations, and with the European and Atlantic institutions, as compared with the geographical departments which are responsible for most of the old-fashioned country-to-country diplomacy.

In these circumstances, it is not surprising that one gets the impression that the Foreign Office has throughout been strained to the limit of its capacities. The limitations imposed upon the size of its staff at home, and particularly abroad, have been put forward as a principal answer to the charge occasionally made that it has been kept inadequately informed by the embassies of some aspects of affairs in particular countries that it needs to know about. If embassies are to be able to cover every important branch of activity in the countries concerned, they will require larger staffs, including a greater variety of specialists, and a decision in favour of this expansion of their responsibilities has never, in fact, been taken. Lack of available staff at home has also been given as the reason why little has been done in the way of building up machinery for long-range planning, either as regards the duties and functioning of the office itself, or in reference to the kind of international problems it may have to face in the future. The experience in Britain would seem not unlike that suggested by American analogies, namely that even if an attempt is made to detach people from day-to-day work so that they can devote themselves to long-range thinking, the increased and increasing burdens on the office will inevitably force their recall to current operations.

It looks, to the outsider, as though the Foreign Office, or rather the Foreign Secretaries, of the period might have been rather bolder in claiming greater resources. But those familiar with the Whitehall machine tend to feel that the Foreign Office is slightly on the defensive as regards its own financial claims in competition with those of the main spending departments. Why this should be so is not entirely clear except, perhaps, for the difficulty of translating diplomatic activity into tangible and measurable forms. But the facts must be taken as they are. Nor should we under-estimate the change that has come over the foreign service in the period. By 1959 there were a very large number of people working in the economic field which was hardly developed at all before the Second World War.

We have already seen that, at the beginning of the period, the Foreign Office was undergoing a major reorganization consequent upon the reforms set out in the 'Eden White Paper' of 1943 (Cmd. 6420). The principal feature of the new system was the amalgamation, into a unified foreign service, of the Consular and Commercial Diplomatic services and the pre-war Diplomatic service. Further development was necessarily along two lines. The internal organization of the department had to be constantly revised so as to see that the departments into which it is itself divided, apportioned the work between themselves in an equitable and rational manner. Second, its responsibility for overseas representation had to be adapted to the needs of the new international organizations, which meant multiplying delegations, including persons on secondment from other departments, as contrasted with traditional embassies. It also meant, of course, the working out of correct relationships with the other departments concerned, so that the policies which the latter wished to see forwarded were properly harmonized with the general objectives of the nation's foreign policy looked at as a whole.

It is important to note that the creative period with regard to the international institutions with which we are concerned fell within Ernest Bevin's tenure of the post of Foreign Secretary. This made it certain that the point of view of the Foreign Office, with which he undoubtedly identified himself, was given its full weight by the Government, in whose counsels he played so prominent a role. It was certainly during his period of office that the economic sections of the Foreign Office underwent their major expansion. Indeed, it has been suggested in some quarters that they were more important then in actually determining policy than they later became when, so it is argued, the economic Departments staged something of a comeback. On the other hand, when a member of the foreign service was, in 1956, made Joint Permanent Secretary to the Treasury on the economic side, this was taken by some people as showing the importance that the economic side of the Foreign Office had now permanently acquired.

The Foreign Office showed throughout the period a remarkable capacity for adapting its organization very rapidly indeed to the successive demands made upon it. The principle governing the allocation of work between departments, the creation of new departments or the amalgamation of existing ones, was the familiar one that the head of the department should be able adequately to supervise all its work. Such flexibility was assisted by the fact that the re-allocation of duties within the department is within the discretion of the Foreign Office itself. Treasury approval is only required when additions to the total establishment are made.

No particular provisions were made for handling the problems created by the necessity of organizing delegations to the new international organizations. These were looked at rather, at any rate at the beginning, as being analogous to new alliances. In allocating personnel, however, the Foreign Office had to take into account simultaneously the importance of the machinery of co-ordination in London. It might be content to limit its representation on a particular delegation, provided that it was strongly represented on the relevant inter-departmental committee at home.

The methods of work developed in the international organizations also involved tremendous burdens upon the home governments. It is technically very difficult to see that fifteen or so representatives of separate sovereign states get their instructions from home in time for a particular meeting. The British system, partly because of its compactness as compared, for instance, with the position in Washington, did prove highly effective in this respect—and this fact was generally noted and admired.

The organization of the Foreign Office in the immediately post-war period, was complicated by the number of questions that had to be dealt with which arose out of the occupation of ex-enemy countries. The Economic Relations Department which, as we have seen, was something which had hardly existed before the war, now worked on a variety of general economic, financial and supply questions, and was deeply involved with bilateral commercial and financial negotiations of great importance, at a time when much essential trade was still managed or controlled by the Government. The superintending under-secretary for this department had also, until 1947, an economic and industrial planning staff to supervise; this staff was concerned with the inter-departmental planning of long-term economic policy towards the ex-enemy countries. In addition, of course, the traditional geographical departments of the Foreign Office were directly concerned with countries which were members of the new organizations. In this respect, the work of the Western Department was central.

Between the end of the war and April or May 1946, there was also a Reconstruction Department which dealt, among other things, with general questions of political and military collaboration with our wartime allies, with the liquidation of the League of Nations and with matters relating to the United Nations Organization and the ILO. The development of the United Nations led to the creation of the post of the permanent United Kingdom representative to that organization—a post filled by the head of the Reconstruction Department which was now wound up. At the same time, that is May 1946, the United Nations Department was set up within the Foreign Office. The business of this department was to deal with general policy towards the United Nations, including the co-ordination of this policy with other departments and with all questions of machinery, procedure and personnel arising out of Britain's membership of that body. Furthermore, the United Nations Department dealt with the organization of international security under the Charter, with the control and regulation of armaments (in conjunction with the Services Liaison Department) and with trusteeship, and international, social and labour questions, with the relationship to specialized agencies within the United Nations and with the International Court of Justice. Questions arising out of the British membership of the International Bank and the International Monetary Fund were, however, the responsibility of the Economic Relations Department.

In May 1947, the United Nations Department was split into two parts: the United Nations (Political) and the United Nations (Economic and Social) Departments. The first of these dealt with general policy, the machinery and administration of the United Nations Secretariat, the organization of international security, control and regulation of armaments, trusteeship, and relations with the International Court of Justice and the Atomic Energy Commission of the United Nations. The Economic and

Social Department dealt with the Economic and Social Council of UNO, with UNESCO generally, with international social and labour questions and with the relations of the United Nations to other inter-governmental agencies.

The Foreign Office side of the negotiations arising out of the Marshall Plan was originally handled in the Economic Relations Department, but early in 1948, this became too much of a burden and unsuited to a department primarily concerned with bilateral negotiations. There was also the problem of maintaining contact with and giving instructions to the permanent delegation to OEEC, the existence of which had not originally been foreseen. It was therefore decided to set up a new department, known as the European Recovery Department, specifically to deal with this new form of multilateral negotiation. This department dealt with both OEEC and ECE.

When, however, the Brussels Treaty Organization was set up in March 1948, it was treated as a regional political combination and responsibility for dealing with it was consequently placed in the Western Department. The North Atlantic Treaty Organization created in the following year, was regarded as a development of the Brussels Treaty Organization and also fell to be dealt with by the Western Department. It is curious to note that the Council of Europe, which came into being in the same year, was put into the sphere of the United Nations (Political) Department despite its regional character.

This arrangement did not last long, since the multiplication of these new international organizations made necessary the creation of a new department—the Western Organizations Department—which dealt with the North Atlantic Treaty Organization, the Brussels Treaty Organization and also the Council of Europe.

The problem of seeing that the Commonwealth interest was properly represented in deliberations dealing with foreign policy, seems to have exercised the Foreign Office at this time, and a special Commonwealth Liaison Department was set up in 1950. This experiment was not a success, since it meant that information, instead of going directly to the Commonwealth Relations Office, went to it at second-hand through this department, which was not treated as being of great importance in view of its lack of executive responsibility. In 1952 it was abolished and the Foreign Office departments concerned, again dealt directly with the CRO.

As we saw earlier, the critical situation created by the outbreak of the Korean War and fears about the situation in Europe, led to a blurring of the lines between American aid directed at promoting Europe's economic recovery and assistance in Europe's rearmament. In December 1950, the European Recovery Department was replaced by the Mutual Aid Department, which was made responsible not only for OEEC and ECE, but also for the economic work of the Council of Europe, in so far as this existed, and more important, for the economic work of NATO. Judging by the arbitrary yardstick of dispatches received, the Mutual Aid Department did roughly the same amount of work as its predecessor.

The Western Organizations Department was given the responsibility for keeping in touch with the negotiations for setting up a European Defence Community, and when these failed and the Brussels Treaty Organization was transformed into WEU, it remained the responsibility of the same department. By 1956, the international organizations had become so important that the Western Department (which for three years 1952–4 had been amalgamated with the Southern Department but was now again a separate one) was considered to have too little work left to do and, in consequence, the Western Organizations Department was amalgamated with it. It was, however, not merely on this occasion a question of distributing the work load. It was almost impossible to distinguish between the respective responsibilities of the two departments. Matters like the reunification of Germany or 'disengagement', which were central to Anglo-German relations, came up again and again in NATO, and it was only logical that the same Foreign Office department should deal with both.

By 1959 the departments in the Foreign Office mainly concerned with the European and Atlantic Organizations were: the Mutual Aid Department, the Western Department, the Economic Relations Department and the Cultural Relations Department. The Mutual Aid Department was responsible for the economic organizations and for all questions dealing with European economic integration, including questions of migration and manpower, for aid from the United States, in as far as this was still a factor, and for security controls on east-west trade which was closely related to it.[1] The Western Department was, as we have seen by now, responsible for all the Western Organizations of a primarily political kind. The Economic Relations Department was responsible for general economic questions, for GATT, the International Monetary Fund, the International Bank, and for liaison with certain other international economic organizations, and for seeing that the Commonwealth economic interests were looked after in the framing of British policy.

The Cultural Relations Department was generally responsible for the educational and cultural interests of Britain abroad, since it maintained close liaison with the British Council and dealt with UNESCO, except in regard to its constitutional, administrative and financial aspects, which were the affair of the United Nations Department. In the context of the present study, the important thing was the department's responsibility for the British share of the cultural and educational work of the European organizations.

An important part of the Foreign Office machinery, from the point of view of inter-departmental co-ordination, was, from 1950, the Permanent Under-Secretary's Department, which was responsible for liaison with the Ministry of Defence, the Chiefs of Staff Organization, and the Joint Intelligence Committee. Until 1958 it also dealt with atomic energy. But in that year a new Atomic Energy and Disarmament Department was created.

We have already noted that the pressure upon the Foreign Office made it difficult for it to deal with long-term planning. The Research Department, which had largely sprung from duties undertaken in wartime, was given increased responsibilities towards the end of our period. By this time the Foreign Office was recruiting specialists for this department and bringing in senior experts concerned with areas which were thought to be of special importance. The department now produced forward-looking papers, containing estimates of future developments, as well as acting in the nature of a reference department

[1] This has subsequently been replaced by the European Economic Organizations Department which deals with OEEC, the ECE, the ECSC, the EEC and related questions and the economic work of NATO. See Lord Strang, 'Inside the Foreign Office', *International Relations*, April 1960.

upon which the other sections of the office could call. It had no policy-making responsibilities; but an attempt was made on two occasions during our period to make arrangements, independent of the Research Department, for forward-looking planning, with the idea of seeing that matters brought up by the Research Department, or noted as significant elsewhere in the office, got proper attention, and to make analysis of policy on a long-term basis. The second experiment of this kind was still in being in 1959. It had involved the formation of a small planning and co-ordination section in the Permanent Under-Secretary's Department. Under the supervision of a Steering Committee, composed of the senior members of the office, this section carried out policy planning and other duties, independently of the Research Department, and also served to co-ordinate the work of the latter with that of the rest of the office on the major problems of the day. Nevertheless, it would obviously be wrong to imagine that any internal reorganization within the Foreign Office could enable plans for a number of years ahead to be made, and this was particularly the case in our period in relation to the European Organizations, since Continental opinion seemed to be evolving at an unexpectedly rapid pace.

The contacts between the United Kingdom Government and international organizations are largely maintained through permanent delegations accredited to the particular organization in question. The composition of these delegations will vary, of course, according to the functions of the organization to which they are accredited, but they differ, generally speaking, from ordinary embassies in that they have a number of officers seconded from what are properly speaking domestic departments. The staffing of such delegations raises a number of important questions.

Is it desirable that the delegation should contain experts on all the questions likely to come up, or can it rely upon bringing people rapidly from London to deal with issues as they arise? Which department should be responsible for nominating the head of the delegation? Should contacts with the home departments be maintained exclusively through the head of the delegation, or should its members retain their own channels of communication with their home departments? What problems, if any, arise from the presence of more than one delegation in a foreign city, or in the relations between the delegations and the embassy to the government of the country in which the particular organization is located?

Some of the questions raised are, of course, akin to those which relate to the foreign service generally, such as the appropriate tour of duty. But it may be asked whether such service demands particular qualities from the members of the foreign service or the home departments who staff it, and whether any particular questions with regard to their selection or training arise.

It has undoubtedly been of great importance that the delegations should attract officers of high quality, both from the foreign service and from the home civil service. With regard to the latter there was, for some time, a considerable degree of friction arising from the fact that members of embassies were regarded as having more representational functions than members of delegations and, therefore, as requiring larger allowances. This was taken in some quarters to mean that the Government attached more importance to embassy than to delegation personnel. However, moves towards a harmonization of allowances have been made in recent years, and these are now determined by a consideration of the work that has to be done and without regard to the question of whether the particular officer is on an embassy staff or delegation. For these reasons this question may be considered a closed one.

On the other hand, it is understandable that non-members of the foreign service may feel that accepting positions on delegations may lead to them getting outside the main stream of promotion. And they may also object to the effect upon their families of an uprooting which would be taken as normal by foreign service officers. Definite efforts have been made to make certain that those who do accept these assignments should be led to feel that their chances of promotion will actually be enhanced through this additional experience. These considerations have not, of course, applied to the foreign service proper, for there the work is considered just as interesting and in many cases more interesting than the work in many conventional embassies. It has been the experience of officers seconded to the NATO delegation (or for that matter to the NATO International Secretariat) that they have not been handicapped on their return to other duty, rather the contrary.

The first of the delegations to be considered is that to OEEC, which was set up in April 1948 under a member of the foreign service who had previously served in the Treasury. Its original establishment was nine, but it went up to seventeen in the years of peak activity, 1949 and 1950, falling again to fourteen in 1952. On June 30, 1952, the first head of the delegation was succeeded by his previous deputy who had held that position on secondment from the Treasury to the Foreign Office since the setting up of the delegation itself.

From July 1, 1952, to March 1954, the NATO and OEEC delegations were regarded as a single organization for internal administrative purposes. In practice, however, this amounted to little more than their having a combined registry and typing pool. The work of the two halves of the delegation remained separate and, in March 1954, the head of the OEEC delegation was accorded the personal rank of ambassador. Certain technical services remained common but the separation was made complete when, early in 1960, the NATO delegation was moved to its new premises in the new NATO building itself.

It is therefore correct to regard the history of the delegation to OEEC as having been continuous from April 1948 despite these formal changes. The work of this delegation is, of course, primarily economic, but its personnel is recruited for it through the Foreign Office. In 1959, leaving aside the head of the delegation, there were seven foreign service officers including the Minister. The Board of Trade supplied two Counsellors and two First Secretaries, the Inland Revenue a Counsellor and the Ministry of Agriculture and Fisheries a First Secretary.

The head of this delegation has from the formal point of view reported to the Foreign Office. For most of the period this has meant the Mutual Aid Department. There has also, of course, been the regular flow of reporting to the chairman of the relevant interdepartmental committee in London whose importance has been stressed earlier on. Finally, there is, of course, the semi-official correspondence on technical questions that goes on directly between the members of the delegation and the relevant Whitehall departments.

In the early stages of OEEC the delegation comprised an Ambassador, three Ministers and three or four Counsellors and much negotiation at a high level was conducted wholly by the delegation itself, for instance, the negotiations for the creation of the European Payments Union. This form of organization was, however, more suitable to the early tasks of the OEEC when it was necessary to work against time in order to secure the appropriations from Marshall Aid.

Later on the OEEC itself, with the strong support of the head of the British delegation, preferred to have regular meetings with senior officials from the capitals so that the Governments should be more directly implicated in the work. High level experts are thus now sent over from London for important meetings. For instance, the Treasury is directly represented on the managing board of the European Monetary Agreement. The delegation provides alternates for such officials, who can deal with the current business between the meetings attended by officials from the capitals. This, however, does not mean that the important work is now done by the visitors and the routine work only by the delegation. The permanent delegate, which in the British case often means his deputy since the delegate himself is Chairman of the OEEC Council, has to deal with all questions of substance arising from the work of the technical committees and has finally to commit his Government in the Executive Committee and in the Council. It is, of course, also the case that the Council may meet at ministerial level, when it will be attended by the Chancellor of the Exchequer and the President of the Board of Trade. It is felt that these arrangements give the maximum of flexibility and enable the status of the countries' representatives at a particular meeting to be determined by the importance of the work to be done.

The ordinary tour of duty on the OEEC delegation has been about two years, which is perhaps rather shorter than that in most embassies. The head of the delegation has not, however, been subject to this rotation, since it is thought that he should stay for a longer period in order to build up his contacts and create confidence in his authority. Between 1948 and 1960, in fact, the delegation from the United Kingdom to the OEEC had only two heads.

The shortness of the tour of duty of the other members of the delegation has been criticized on the grounds that although this keeps the delegation in touch with thinking in the home departments, it weakens its ability to report successfully upon trends in the OEEC itself. The view of the OEEC Secretariat is that three or four years would be the desirable maximum, since members of the delegation staying for a longer period than this would indeed get too out of touch with thinking at home to be useful. The British have, of course, the advantage, particularly as compared with some of the smaller countries, in always being able to produce someone from within the Government service who has the particular degree of specialized economic knowledge required for the matter in hand. Other countries may have to call upon private industry which presents obvious difficulties.

From the point of view of a department like the Board of Trade, it is essential, when things have to be done, that persons should be sent over from London and there is, in fact, a good deal of movement to and fro. Other countries go further than Britain in using senior persons from departments at home rather than their permanent representatives. This is not only because of the fact that they have fewer people, but partly because their trading interests as a whole are less important so that the European side bulks larger.

The early history of the delegation to NATO is more difficult to reconstruct because of the long period of uncertainty as to the precise structure and functions of the organization itself. It was only in April 1952 that the minister's deputy became the first holder of the post of permanent representative to NATO. At this time, as we have seen, there was some overlapping between the work of NATO and that of OEEC and the two delegations were formally regarded as one. For instance, the permanent representative's deputy on the NATO Council, who looked after the economic side of NATO, still held his previous position as Chairman of the Economic Committee of OEEC though he was now a part of the NATO delegation and not of the delegation to OEEC. However, by 1954 the spheres of the two organizations and of the delegations to them were clearly demarcated.

If the economic overlap need cause no difficulty, there is another one arising out of the fact that NATO is both a political and a military organization. All its work is, however, under a single supreme body, namely the Council. For most of the time it is the permanent representatives who sit on the Council and who are representatives of their governments, being responsible for dealing with military as well as political questions. The delegation which stood at the figure of fourteen officers by early 1957 is, technically speaking, a Foreign Office delegation and all its members are seconded to the Foreign Office for the duration of their tour of duty. For most practical purposes it is run on Foreign Office lines, although in its composition it represents something of a microcosm of Whitehall itself and has indeed to take a very broad view of its activities. Apart from the members of the foreign service, who included the three successive heads of the delegation in our period, it includes members seconded from the Ministry of Defence, who may themselves very likely be members of one or other of the service departments, with only a short period of experience at the Ministry of Defence before joining the delegation. Other departments also second officers. At the end of 1959 the Treasury and the Ministry of Aviation were represented on the delegation and there had previously been officers from the Ministry of Transport. Because of the easy access to London, it is possible to keep the delegation small and, as in the case of OEEC, to afforce it as the need arises. On the ministerial level the Foreign Secretary has come to be the normal representative though, as we have seen, the Minister of Defence, the Chancellor of the Exchequer and even the Prime Minister may on occasion attend. Of the official members, one of those seconded from the Ministry of Defence is an establishment expert and represents the United Kingdom on the Military Budget Committee and the Civil Budget Committee of NATO.

The delegation reports to the Foreign Office and its contacts are with various departments within it, though the Western Department (as formerly the Western Organizations Department) has co-ordinating and centralizing functions. There is, in addition, a good deal of semi-official correspondence between members of the delegation and other Whitehall departments.

On certain aspects of the delegation's work the relevant telegrams may actually be drafted in the Ministry of Defence although they are sent via Foreign Office channels. It would be possible for the principal member of the NATO delegation seconded from the Ministry of Defence, to get his instructions directly from that Ministry, but this is avoided because of the necessity of keeping the other departments in London concerned with NATO affairs fully informed. The channelling of instructions through the Foreign Office also helps to keep other British missions abroad informed about the work of NATO. There is, of course, in addition, constant and close informal consultation between the Foreign Office and the Ministry of Defence.

The tour of duty of those seconded from the service departments is three years, as it would be in the Ministry of Defence itself. The argument for keeping the tour short is once more that it is important that members of the delegation should be in close touch with the development of thought at home.

It is, of course, true that much of the multilateral work of an organization like NATO requires to be buttressed by bilateral contacts with other delegations. This gives particular significance to the relations between the delegation and the embassy to the country in which the organization is located, in this case France. Adequate liaison arrangements are made with the various embassy attachés, whose work covers a similar field to that of the delegation, and, on an informal basis, the head of the press and propaganda section of the embassy also works for the NATO delegation. It is part of the duties of the head of the delegation to see that the embassy is kept fully informed of anything that transpires which is likely to affect its own work.

When we come to the military side of NATO, we must again emphasize that the delegation is very closely concerned with the work of the Standing Group, the Military Committee and the various commanders. Their papers are received and commented on in the delegation, and the questions they raise for decision have to be settled in the Council.

There is a British national military representative at SHAPE who is a serving officer with two subordinates representing the other two services. The national military representative and his staff are not attached to the delegation in the way that service attachés are attached to an embassy, but it has been agreed with the chiefs of staff that they do, in fact, act in that capacity in addition to their other duties. The national military representatives are there, it must be emphasized, to represent their chiefs of staff directly and have no political functions. Nevertheless, the contacts of the delegation with the national military representatives are probably even closer than those maintained by an ordinary ambassador with his service attachés. The national military representative attends the regular meetings of the delegation and supplies it with military information which may be particularly useful because of the fact that intelligence in NATO comes exclusively from national sources. On the other hand, the delegation gives to the national military representative, and through him to the senior British officers at SHAPE, general political information and guidance. Furthermore, the head of the delegation may often be in a position to obtain important military information directly from SACEUR and the other senior commanders. SACEUR's political contacts are thus with the Secretary-General of NATO and with the individual members of the Council.

Much of the central military machinery of the alliance is, of course, centred not in Paris but in Washington. As has been seen, the senior military organ of NATO under the Council, is the Military Committee of the national chiefs of staff. This body meets only rarely and the main military work is done by the Military Committee in Permanent Session. The working organ of both these bodies is the Standing Group through whom the military instructions go to the NATO senior commanders and from whom military advice comes to the Council. The United Kingdom is represented by a senior serving officer on the Military Committee and on the Standing Group. This officer is also the head of the Joint Services Mission to the United States. He is not a member of the embassy staff though he acts as military adviser to the ambassador. This officer reports to and gets directions from the chiefs of staff and the Ministry of Defence. Political questions arising in the course of his work are taken up by the Ministry of Defence directly with the Foreign Office in London.

It will thus be seen that from the point of view of the British involvement in NATO as a whole, the essential instrument is the delegation and its head.

We next come to the delegation to the European Coal and Steel Community, which was originally established at Luxembourg in September 1952. Its first head was a business man with civil service experience who was assisted by a representative from the Ministry of Fuel and Power and an under-secretary from the Ministry of Supply, who was joined in 1953 by another member of that department. The deputy to the head of the delegation acted as head of Chancery. This organization lasted until 1955. Assessors to the delegation were appointed from the two industries. On the steel side these came first from the Iron and Steel Federation, and later from the Steel Board as it was reconstituted after denationalization.

When the Treaty of Association between the United Kingdom and the ECSC came into force in September 1955, the delegation was cut down to two persons: its head, coming from the Foreign Office, and his deputy. There were two expert advisers, one from the Coal Board and the other from the Steel Board. The delegation did not play any important part in the making of British policy but was there to gather information and to negotiate in accordance with instructions received from Whitehall.

The delegation, like others, reports to the Foreign Office, though in the period when the Treaty of Association was being worked out it also reported to the inter-departmental committee under Treasury chairmanship which was considering these questions. Since the Treaty came into effect, most of its work has involved contact with the Coal and Steel Boards. The Ministry of Power has become less concerned than formerly.

The head of the United Kingdom delegation was accredited to Euratom as well in July 1958, and in September of that year was made responsible for maintaining informal liaison with the European Economic Community. In January 1959, a permanent office for the delegation was opened in Brussels. Its staff included an expert adviser from the United Kingdom Atomic Energy Authority. The Brussels office remained under the supervision of the head of the delegation who continued to reside in Luxembourg.

One may add, though this brings us beyond our period, that the head of this delegation was accredited as representative to all three European Communities at the end of 1959 and took up permanent residence in Brussels in the following year.

In addition to NATO the British Government has to work with a number of international organizations which have their headquarters in Washington, and this makes the Washington embassy itself, in some respects, more similar to a delegation than to a normal embassy. There is, for instance, the British alternate for the Chancellor of the Exchequer on the governing bodies of the International Monetary Fund and the World Bank. In 1952–54, this official, who had formerly been head of the British delegation to OEEC, had two deputies, one for the Bank who came from the Treasury and one for the Fund who was seconded from the Bank of England. This officer was not part of the embassy at that time. The Washington embassy had an Economic Minister, and in 1951 the new holder of this position was also made head of the British Treasury and Supply Delegation. This arrangement was considered a weakness because of the close connection between the work of the Bank and the International Monetary Fund, and the general financial policies of the United States.

When a new ambassador was appointed in 1954 the arrangement was altered. The ambassador had had previous experience of this kind of problem when serving in Washington from 1945 to 1947. At that time he had assisted the ambassador of the time, Lord Halifax, in the work of co-ordinating the different missions, supply, food and raw materials. The new arrangement he now made was that his Economic Minister (who was a merchant banker by profession) should also function as the chancellor's deputy on the governing bodies of the Bank and Fund. He was responsible to the ambassador for the political aspects of this work, while the system of having two deputies for himself was retained.

The general arrangement, therefore, in Washington is that there is a special representative of every Whitehall department concerned in some way in international activity. But although these officers have the right to correspond on technical matters with their departments, without reference to the diplomatic side of the embassy, they are, nevertheless, members of the embassy staff and are responsible to the ambassador on all matters of policy which could affect the general relations between the United Kingdom and the United States. There are minor similarities between this situation and that in Paris where, for instance, the commercial minister is the British representative on the board of the Suez Canal Company. But of course the much greater size of the delegations to the OEEC and NATO, as compared with the specialized work done in Washington, makes it impossible to co-ordinate all British activity in Paris under a single ambassador.

For the sake of completeness, although it falls outside the framework of this inquiry, reference should be made to the questions raised by the existence in New York of the British delegation to the United Nations. The work of the Washington embassy and of this delegation are, in fact, quite separate. But the ambassador and the head of the delegation both have to do much public relations work and have to ensure, through informal arrangements, that there is no conflict between what they say.

Finally, one might raise the general problem of the effect of the existence of these delegations upon the work of the embassies themselves. It is true that in a sense they do work which would otherwise fall on the embassies. For instance, the negotiations for the proposed Free Trade Area might have been handled by the ambassadors instead of within the framework of OEEC. But, as we have pointed out in relation to NATO, the organizations themselves tend to throw up new problems for solution by the embassies in the sense that they come across questions which can only be resolved through direct negotiation with the particular countries concerned. Although, therefore, there has been some redistribution of diplomatic activity, it would probably be untrue to say that the existence of these delegations has diminished the burdens upon embassies, certainly where the larger countries are concerned. Some smaller embassies have decreased in importance—The Hague and Brussels, for instance, with the coming into existence of the North Atlantic Council.

CHAPTER 6

The Impact upon the Departments

It is, of course, impossible to discuss any aspect of British policy without keeping in mind the fact that the United Kingdom is the centre of a Commonwealth of independent countries. It is, at the same time, still responsible in varying degrees for a number of dependent territories. In the period with which we are concerned a number of territories were progressing from the latter to the former position and this helped to complicate the arrangements for dealing with their affairs in the relevant Government departments at home.

It may be asked, as a preliminary to considering these arrangements in relation to the international organizations we are concerned with, whether the Commonwealth itself should be regarded as another international organization of which Britain is a member. Do the habits of consultation and co-operation between the Commonwealth countries amount to a formal arrangement?[1] It would, I think, be generally agreed that the answer to this question is in the negative. The Commonwealth is more than the sum of the relations of the independent states of which it is composed. One official with much experience of Commonwealth relations in recent times has described the Commonwealth as 'a collection of states which although independent are not foreign'. And this must do.

The general view in the Foreign Office appears to be that the Commonwealth, having no common policies as distinct from the policies of its individual members, cannot be regarded as a unit, and that therefore its members have no right to be consulted automatically on any and every issue of British policy that comes up. The degree of consultation with the individual members will

[1] This problem, like several others raised in the following pages, is discussed in J. D. B. Miller, *The Commonwealth and the World* (London, 1958).

vary according to the particular problem involved. Since the most important examples of the influence of Commonwealth countries in our period have mainly concerned Asian affairs, this aspect of policy does not bulk as large for our present purposes as it might have done were we reviewing the full range of British commitments abroad.

Nevertheless, the development of Commonwealth consultation is worth chronicling here if only as part of the setting within which the European arrangements were made. In addition to the frequent meetings of Commonwealth Prime Ministers in the period, there was some specific development of consultative machinery, in particular, after the two meetings of Commonwealth Finance Ministers in 1952. This form of consultation was reviewed at the Commonwealth Trade and Economic Conference at Montreal in 1958. The Conference put on record its agreement that the machinery was working well, was flexible and informal and 'well fitted to the family character of the Commonwealth relationship'. It decided to set up a Commonwealth Economic Consultative Council which would, at its highest level, consist of the Finance and Economic Ministers of the Commonwealth countries meeting together whenever circumstances so demanded. The Council was to incorporate the various elements and bodies through which such economic consultation was already taking place and any further ones that might be set up. It was agreed that meetings at high official level would also be held when necessary to prepare for the meetings of ministers.[1]

These Commonwealth consultations, it is emphasized by those who have taken part in them, differ from those of international institutions largely by reason of the greater flexibility referred to in the Montreal communiqué. It is felt that Commonwealth leaders and officials can discuss matters with their colleagues in other Commonwealth countries on the same friendly basis as do ministers and officials within the governmental structure of the United Kingdom itself. On the other hand, of course, such discussions are not held for the purpose of reaching agreed policies to be put forward by a single governmental system. It is merely a question of reaching the maximum consensus of opinion between independent States,

[1] See Cmnd. 539 (1958).

and for any concerted action it is obvious that unanimity is required.

The same general considerations apply to any consultations undertaken between themselves by representatives of Commonwealth countries abroad. A former British ambassador to the United States has put it on record that the ambassadors of the Commonwealth countries in Washington in his time used to meet at regular fortnightly intervals to discuss matters of common interest even when these were the subject of direct disagreement between them.[1]

In the earlier part of the period the most important aspect of the Commonwealth relationship on the economic side was probably the sterling area. Though this, of course, both excluded Canada and included a number of non-Commonwealth countries. But as sterling approached nearer to full convertibility and as discrimination in Britain in favour of sterling sources of supply was reduced, this aspect of Commonwealth consultation tended to give way to problems of trade and development as shown, for instance, in the balance of the report of the Montreal Conference. The affairs of the sterling area were watched over by the meetings of the finance ministers, usually held annually. For some years these came immediately after the annual meetings of the International Bank and the International Monetary Fund. But the 1959 meeting of the finance ministers was held beforehand, and the same arrangement was made for 1960.

The United Kingdom Government, as the holder of the central gold and dollar reserves and the main source of sterling capital, produces a report on the past year's functioning of the area with such recommendations as seem desirable from the point of view of keeping up the level of the reserves. Agreements made in pursuance of such recommendations seem to have been kept, and those concerned with the system consider that it has functioned successfully.

Between these periodical meetings at high level, the day-to-day work of the machinery of the Sterling Area was, until 1955, shared between two bodies in London—the Commonwealth Liaison Committee and the Sterling Area Statistical Committee. All the Commonwealth members were represented on each of these committees, despite the fact that Canada has never been a

[1] Sir Oliver Franks in the *Listener*, November 18, 1954.

member of the Sterling Area. In 1955 the Sterling Area Committee disappeared, its work being taken over by the Commonwealth Liaison Committee.[1]

Commonwealth co-operation in a more limited field has also been exemplified by the Colombo Plan organization, for this sprang from a wholly Commonwealth initiative, and its flexibility and consultative methods are essentially those of the Commonwealth, even though the United States of America and many non-Commonwealth Asian countries have joined it since it began.

It is when we come to the major fields of defence policy and foreign policy that the limitations of the Commonwealth relationship can more clearly be seen. The Commonwealth countries are free to pursue their own foreign policy and make such arrangements for co-operative defence as they find desirable. Here the international organizations that they may belong to, such as NATO, CENTO or SEATO, are more important than the fact of Commonwealth membership. Nevertheless, Britain helps all of them with training facilities and scientific information, so that at the professional level there is a considerable degree of consultation and joint activity even as between the United Kingdom and the older Commonwealth countries, on the one hand, and a country like India, which belongs to none of the alliances. Even so, of course, the Ministry of Defence has hardly any contact with India and Ceylon and not much with South Africa, while, because of the pacts, it has close links with Pakistan, Australia and New Zealand. The Commonwealth Relations Office has a direct liaison with the British Chiefs of Staff Organization. The Commonwealth Relations Office, as the channel for all official communications between the Government of the United Kingdom and the other members of the Commonwealth, is indeed central to the whole position. The organization of the CRO includes a foreign affairs division which comprises the following departments: South Asia, United Nations, Defence, West and Middle East, Far East and Pacific.

A very important aspect of the work of keeping the Commonwealth informed about developments in Britain's position consists of a regular flow of telegrams, forwarded to the

---

[1] On the machinery of Commonwealth consultation generally see Heather Harvey, *Consultation and Co-operation in the Commonwealth* (London, 1952); Patrick Maitland, *A Task for Giants* (London, 1957).

Commonwealth capitals by the CRO through the several High Commissioners. These telegrams both serve as a vehicle for information and permit a regular exchange about the views and intentions of Commonwealth governments. Finally, there are the very important telegrams exchanged directly by the Prime Minister with Commonwealth Prime Ministers.

The Foreign Office has had to concern itself with its own role in this activity. In 1947 it set up a special Commonwealth Liaison Department but this was abolished in April 1952. It was felt that the existence of such a special department meant that information was passed on by persons with only a second-hand knowledge of the particular problems. Keeping the Commonwealth countries informed is now the responsibility of the persons in the Foreign Office directly concerned with the matters in question.

High Commissioners in London and their staffs, at all levels, have direct access to the Foreign Office, as indeed they have to all other United Kingdom Government Departments. Telegrams, whether of information or for action, which pass between the Foreign Office and British diplomatic missions abroad in either direction are repeated by the senders to High Commissioners overseas, likely to be concerned. These may be for the information of the High Commissioner only, or he may be instructed to repeat the contents to the Commonwealth Government to which he is accredited.

In this connection the following statement from an official source is worth bearing in mind:

'As befits the relationship between Member countries of the Commonwealth, relations are maintained on a less formal, freer and more intimate basis than is usual between foreign governments. In consequence the range of contacts between UK High Commissioners and the Commonwealth governments to which they are accredited is of a very extensive nature covering almost every aspect of Government policy, since it is vital to the intimacy of the Commonwealth relationship that on all matters of common concern there should be the greatest possible measure of exchange of information, community of view and co-operation in action.'[1]

[1] *Third Report* from the Select Committee on Estimates (CRO), July 15, 1959, Section 11.

There are other methods also by which the Commonwealth countries are kept informed. A minister or a senior official from the Foreign Office may attend a meeting at the CRO between the Secretary for Commonwealth Relations and the Commonwealth High Commissioners. Occasionally, members of the foreign service are appointed to serve on the staffs of British High Commissioners in Commonwealth countries and, more rarely, members of the Commonwealth service serve in British embassies abroad. In addition to the CRO representative on the permanent United Nations Delegation, who has First Secretary rank, the CRO supplies a similarly ranking official to the embassy in Washington. It looks as though the interchange between the foreign service and the Commonwealth service is looked at with favour on both sides and is likely to increase.

Britain is also concerned to see that the new Commonwealth countries have adequate representation abroad, and new entrants to their foreign services do an initial course of training in London together with entrants to the British foreign service and Commonwealth service.

We have earlier alluded to the existence of the permanent committee of Commonwealth officials in London called the Commonwealth Liaison Committee. There have been suggestions for promoting this body into one capable of securing some degree of day-to-day co-ordination in economic policy between the Commonwealth countries, but these have not come to much, largely because their governments naturally prefer to reserve such matters for decision at home. The Committee, therefore, which meets once a fortnight or once a month serves, for the most part, the modest though useful purpose of providing the Commonwealth countries with an up-to-date account of the development of United Kingdom policy, particularly with regard to such questions as are likely to affect their own interests.

Although many Commonwealth governments have had larger staffs in London than the United Kingdom maintains in their capitals, and although these staffs are of a very high quality, the majority of consultative traffic goes through the United Kingdom High Commissioners. In some cases this is because the United Kingdom has a better communications system than the other governments concerned. But generally, since much of the consultation is initiated from London, it is natural to transact it through the United Kingdom representatives if only so as to keep them in touch. In the light of these and other considerations, there has been some discussion as to whether the CRO is an essential part of the mechanism of modern British Government or whether these relations with the Commonwealth countries could not be handled as well by the Foreign Office or, with respect to some matters, by the Overseas Finance Division of the Treasury. Some Commonwealth countries might prefer to see the Foreign Office as the main instrument of communication with them, but with others the United Kingdom has a more intimate and extensive relationship than with foreign countries. It has also been argued that the relatively small CRO and Commonwealth service is preferable, in that the persons concerned in the Commonwealth countries can get to know the people they have to deal with in London more intimately. This is thought to be particularly helpful to the newer Commonwealth countries. Nevertheless, it remains the fact that the major work of the CRO relates to the constitutional development of the Commonwealth itself rather than to its external relations.

Some of the work done for the Commonwealth countries, taken together, is not done by the Commonwealth Relations Department at all. For instance, the Secretariat of the Commonwealth Air Transport Council has been supplied by the Civil Aviation side of the Ministry of Transport. Much of the work has been done informally by this ministry and is now presumably the concern of the new Ministry of Aviation.

These complicated and diffuse relationships make it understandable that people should differ as to whether the Commonwealth relationship is or is not a closer one than that which had developed, in our period, between the United Kingdom and the European countries, with which it is linked through the OEEC and other organizations. Some people feel that the depth of consultation on economic and financial questions reached in the OEEC has been more considerable than that attained in the Commonwealth. The mere fact that the OEEC work is centred in Paris, where meetings at any level can be called together very rapidly, makes for more intensive consultation than the greater distances between the Commonwealth countries would permit. Others assert that through the working of the Commonwealth machinery the officials in the different capitals, without the barrier of language, have got to know one another very well and estimate very rapidly each other's likely reactions to new developments.

What foreign observers will want to know is, of course, the effect of membership of the Commonwealth on Britain's ability to accept certain types of international organization or to follow particular policies within them. Is it the case that the Commonwealth relationship has been the principal obstacle to integration on the lines favoured within the six countries of Little Europe or has the Commonwealth merely provided a smoke-screen for considerations of direct national interest?

As with so many other aspects of the problem, the original discussions over the Coal and Steel Community provide some of the best material for answering questions of this kind. Speaking in the debate on the Schuman Plan in the House of Commons on June 26, 1950, Sir Stafford Cripps said: 'Throughout all this period of intense intra-European activity, we have been able to carry the Commonwealth with us, and we have not in any way sacrificed the interests of the Commonwealth to those of Europe —nor have we done the reverse'—but, of course, things have never been as simple as that. Commonwealth considerations were, as has already been noted, particularly important in determining the limits to which the United Kingdom could go in collaborating with the Coal and Steel Community when it was set up. Steel having been in short supply in the early post-war years, Britain was able to sell it abroad at an export premium which helped to compensate its own steel makers for the home controls. The Commonwealth was not charged the full export premium. Under the Schuman Plan this system of double pricing might have been disallowed, in which case the premium on exports to the Commonwealth would have had to go. The Commonwealth market is of particular importance to the steel industry, absorbing a very high proportion of its output.

It is understandable therefore that by article 9c of the agreement of association between the United Kingdom and the European Coal and Steel Community, the Council of the Association was instructed to have regard to 'the special relationship between the United Kingdom and other members of the Commonwealth of Nations'.

Without pursuing this topic further, it can be stated as a

general rule, of which the above provides one example, that no important departure in policy will be taken by Britain without prior consultation with other Commonwealth countries. The idea of the European Monetary Agreement, for instance, was presented to OEEC by the British Government after it had been cleared with the other Commonwealth Governments. It is not, then, so much that there have been conflicts of interest between the Commonwealth relationship and the European aspects of Britain's policies, as that the United Kingdom has been unwilling to enter into binding agreements which might provoke such conflicts in the future.

In view of these considerations, the necessity for taking the Commonwealth view into account whenever British policy has to be presented in international organizations is obvious. This can be done partly through the CRO, but it is also often advisable that the Treasury representative at such international organizations should have had some experience of the Commonwealth aspects of British affairs. Or again, the Foreign Office may need to be directly represented where Commonwealth policy is discussed at a high level. At the Montreal Conference in 1958, for instance, the senior Foreign Office official who had been working with Mr Maudling on the proposed Free Trade Area negotiations was himself present, and therefore able to report back to the Foreign Office on Commonwealth reactions to the way things had gone.

The work and organization of the Colonial Office has also been affected by the development of international institutions. This, of course, has mainly been the case in regard to the United Nations family of organizations which have very direct interests in dependent communities; but the European organizations have also shown concern with this field. The problems of organization which these developments have presented to the Colonial Office have been met, in part, by expanding the 'subject departments' of the Colonial Office, that is to say, those departments which deal with particular aspects of colonial administration wherever these arise, as opposed to the 'geographical departments' which are organized on a regional basis. According to a recent authoritative account, the subject departments do 'a large body of economic and financial work concerning trade agreements, exchange control, Commonwealth economic conferences, American and other foreign technical assistance and all kinds of activities dealt with by the numerous international organs'.[1] The economic aspects of these may be dealt with according to their subject by the Economic Division or the Social Services Departments.

A more recent development in the Colonial Office has been the creation and expansion of the International Relations Department. Until 1943, there was no department of this kind designed specifically to deal with international organizations and, more particularly, with issues of foreign policy affecting colonial questions. The immediate motive for creating this department arose from the feeling in the Colonial Office that it was essential that its point of view should be represented in dealing with the Foreign Office and other Whitehall departments. It was felt that it was desirable that the British Government should have a unified view on the development of colonial issues, rather than leaving the individual departments to handle them as they arose.

These questions of co-ordinating policy within Whitehall were more prominent at the time than the idea of the direct representation of the Colonial Office in international organizations. There was, however, the direct and immediate issue of the new Trusteeship proposals of the United Nations, which involved the future of the former British mandates. For this reason, a senior Colonial Office official was needed to represent the office in the post-hostilities planning organization. (In the period of the League of Nations the organizational aspects of running the mandates had been dealt with by the General Department, but the reports on the individual territories had fallen to the relevant regional departments.)

In November 1945, there came an attempt to get a measure of Anglo-French co-operation in Africa, which was thought of as being genuinely desirable in the interests of the colonial territories themselves, and not merely as a natural consequence of the close co-operation of the two Governments in European affairs. The French Colonial Office did not, however, approve of the direct contacts established between the two colonial administrations on the spot, and the handling of these questions became the affair of the ordinary channels of diplomatic negotiation.

[1] Sir Charles Jeffries, *The Colonial Office* (London: Allen & Unwin, 1956), p. 175.

The Colonial Office, nevertheless, wished to retain its International Relations Department to deal with international issues arising from colonial questions, and the department was therefore permanently established. This department has mainly concerned itself with political questions. Since there already existed the Economic Division in the Colonial Office, OEEC questions were dealt with there, but on political questions the Economic Division has had to co-operate with the International Relations Department. The Economic Intelligence and Planning Department, as it was called for a time, dealt with Marshall Aid and the Anglo-American economic negotiations in relation to colonial questions, and also with commercial relations and with GATT.

At one period the pressure of work on the International Relations Department led to its being divided into two. This was the consequence of extreme activity on the part of the specialized agencies of the United Nations, particularly UNESCO and FAO, so that the political side of the department which dealt with the United Nations General Assembly had to be divided from the economic side of the department. Since then, however, the department has been reunified. In the Economic Division of the Colonial Office there are Assistant Secretaries specializing in international economic matters, and one of them was particularly concerned with the Free Trade Area negotiations. Generally speaking the organization of the Colonial Office, on a functional as well as a regional basis, had made it possible for it to deal specifically with the issues that affected the different territories for which it is responsible, and enabled it to represent their needs in dealing, for instance, with international organizations such as the World Bank.

A rather different question has been that of the representation of the colonial territories themselves in international organizations. This question first arose in connection with the ILO, which was the only international organization of importance to remain in continuous effective existence through the war period and which, in 1944, was very active and engaged in holding conferences on social policy which involved dependent territories. Because of the previous relationship of the ILO with the League of Nations, the whole question of representation fell to be reconsidered. It was particularly important because of the question of whether international bodies of the ILO type, working through the drafting of conventions, should treat dependent territories as requiring special provision. The Colonial Office developed the idea of having associate members of international organizations, which meant that non-sovereign territories would have a direct voice in the organizations, and not merely supply members to the metropolitan delegations. Such associate members would have all rights other than voting rights. This scheme was first put forward at the World Health Conference in 1946.

The ILO also creates a great deal of work which falls directly on the Social Services Departments of the Colonial Office, but the International Relations Department is called in if any issues of principle emerge.

In a period in which so many territories have been graduating towards full independence within the Commonwealth, it has been important to maintain relations between the Colonial Office and those responsible for the affairs of the Commonwealth as a whole. This has been done either through the International Relations Department or through the Economic Division. For instance, at the Montreal Conference in 1958, the Colonial Office provided an advisory delegation to see that the point of view of the dependent territories was taken into account. Generally speaking, the Colonial Office has retained a very free hand on matters of commercial policy affecting the colonies. Occasionally the Foreign Office has asked for a concession on the colonial side in order to ease a negotiation, but generally speaking it has not interfered. Should a difference of opinion arise between the Colonial Office and the Foreign Office on a matter of this kind, it has either to be settled in an inter-departmental meeting or go direct to the ministers concerned.

A recent writer has suggested that one objection to entering a European union may have been the belief 'that British colonial policy and British relations with her former dependencies would both receive nothing but harm from a closer political association with such notorious "colonialists" as the French, Dutch and Belgians. Britain might not only find herself identified with the policies of these countries, but perhaps called upon to modify her own policy to suit theirs'.[1] It does not appear to be the case that the Colonial Office has ever put forward objections of this kind in relation to proposals for closer association with Europe.

[1] J. D. B. Miller, *The Commonwealth in the World*, p. 108.

Although Britain took the lead in the post-war world in the movement towards giving independence to dependent territories, it was never thought likely that closer association with countries who took a different view would impede this process. It was felt that Britain could well defend and maintain her own point of view. In fact, Britain has maintained close technical co-operation in the colonial field with a number of the countries most directly involved in the movement towards closer integration in Europe. There has, for example, been the work of the Caribbean Commission, the South Pacific Commission and the Commission for technical co-operation in Africa south of the Sahara (CCTA). There was also a fairly regular direct liaison on colonial policy with France and Belgium whose African empires have been contiguous with so much British territory.

It is natural to look next at the impact of the national organizations upon those departments in British Government directly concerned with the problem of defence. It is a commonplace of discussion on defence questions that the mere existence of alliances tends to foster a closer co-ordination of national defence policies in order that the national point of view may be most effectively presented in their councils. In all the major countries, therefore, there has been a tendency to build up a ministry of defence as distinguished from the political heads of service ministries or supply departments, and to this process Britain has, of course, provided no exception.

Generally speaking it is, of course, important in dealing with British Government to distinguish between the powers of the Minister of Defence and the functions of the ministry. The powers of the Minister are not exercised through direct instructions from him to the service ministers, but through the approval and modification of proposals made by inter-service and inter-ministerial committees for which the Ministry of Defence provides the facilities.[1] On the other hand, although the Ministry of Defence is thus mainly occupied in servicing these committees, 'in certain fields it does play a more active role: liaison with NATO, the Commonwealth and other allies is primarily a Ministry of Defence responsibility'.[2]

[1] See Michael Howard, 'Central Defence Organization in Great Britain 1959', *Political Quarterly* (January–March 1960).
[2] *ibid.*, p. 70.

The Ministry of Defence was created before NATO, but its structure has been well suited to coping with the responsibilities put upon it by Britain's membership of the organization. This structure can be regarded as a threefold one. There is the Division of the Chief of the Defence Staff, covering the military side, the Central Division under the Permanent Secretary, which deals with administration and finance and the general policy of the department, and finally, the Department of the Chief Scientist. The work of the whole Ministry is co-ordinated by the Permanent Secretary who is the Minister's principal adviser.

Although there is a division of the Ministry dealing primarily with maintaining contacts with NATO and WEU, other parts of it such as the organization for handling budgetary matters and the research and development section are also closely though not exclusively concerned with NATO. It is therefore the case that there is no single officer in the department working exclusively with NATO, but that there are a large number of persons much of whose time is taken up with the programme side of NATO and with consequential questions of armaments and production. Forward planning is, of course, part of the ministry's function, and one of its divisions responsible to an under-secretary has given much time to working out practical schemes for making a reality of the slogan of inter-dependence. Here again, bilateral contacts, for instance, and indeed, particularly, contacts with the United States, are an important part of the department's work and very directly related to its NATO responsibilities.

In contrast to the relations between the economic departments not much defence work is done through committees. For instance, on the infra-structure side of NATO, one member of the Ministry is responsible for contacts with the three service departments on the technical matters involved and he then instructs the relevant member of the NATO delegation in Paris. This kind of relationship between the Ministry of Defence and the individual service departments is now fairly well stabilized.

With regard to the representation of Britain in the various military aspects of the NATO and WEU machinery and the British contribution to the international staff at SHAPE, there is a balance of advantages and disadvantages. The services may

151

be reluctant to surrender their best men for jobs of this kind while it is necessary on the other hand that the British personnel be as strong as possible. In fact an increasingly large number of service people and civil servants from the Defence Department and service ministries will have had experience of the international machinery for defence. Indeed, this is probably the most important way in which thinking on defence at home is conditioned to take account of the demands of the organizations.

Since it has been claimed that it is the Air Force which has best assimilated the idea of permanent international co-operation in defence, the internal organization of the Air Ministry in this respect may be singled out for notice. Originally a special post was created, that of director of NATO affairs, but it was found that this was not a suitable method of dealing with the problems raised by NATO. The post was, therefore, abolished at the end of 1956. The point is that the organization of the Ministry under the Air Council is a functional one primarily directed towards producing an efficient Air Force. A large number of people, expert in NATO problems and much concerned with them, work in the Ministry, but they are involved in the ordinary business of the departments so that there are no particular parts of the Ministry specifically concerned with NATO affairs. One section of the Ministry working under the Chief of the Air Staff (S.6) is made up of a group of civil servants who are responsible for maintaining continuity and co-ordination throughout the functional organization, and for seeing that the general body of Air Force doctrine, evolved by the staff, is fully appreciated. There is thus little chance that the NATO aspect of things will be overlooked.

In addition there is the circulation of ideas inherent in the fact that the Ministry of Defence's own staff is interchangeable as between the department of the NATO Delegation and with the other Service Departments. The Ministry normally takes in people for three years from the Service Departments to which they then return. The Service Departments are supposed to send to the Ministry men best fitted to deal with policy rather than with pure administration. For the work of the department is specialized and more like the work of the Foreign Office or the Colonial Office than like that of an ordinary administrative department. As we have seen, people are sent either from the

Ministry itself, or after a brief period there to a three-year tour in the delegations. No settled routine for this has been established because the demands of the international organizations are constantly altering. It is felt to be undesirable that people should specialize too much on the international organizations' aspect of defence for fear that they might become too absorbed in technical questions of procedure, instead of concentrating on the policy decisions that need to be made.

When we turn to the economic departments, the Treasury, of course, holds pride of place. As we have already noted, the immediate post-war years marked a recovery in the position of the Treasury as the major economic department after its relative eclipse in wartime. There was a period when the claims of the Foreign Office, as advanced by Mr Bevin, for a major say in foreign economic policy were of considerable importance, for Mr Bevin was regarded as a co-ordinating minister for overseas affairs generally.[1] But with the assumption of major responsibility in the whole field of economic planning by Sir Stafford Cripps, and his subsequent appointment to the Chancellorship of the Exchequer, this period came to an end, and since 1947 the Treasury's primacy has been undisputed.[2] These developments can only be understood in the light of the major expansion which has taken place in the whole of the Government's responsibilities in the economic sphere. Because of the major importance of the balance of payments question for Britain and the various agreements made for dealing with it, as well as the setting up of new international institutions, this new activity on the part of the Government was particularly marked in the field of external economic affairs.

The machinery of exchange control and import licensing was used as part of a general attempt to control the balance of external payments, while inhibiting as little as possible internal economic growth. The responsibility for directing policy was centred in the Overseas Finance Division of the Treasury, which used as its executive arms the Bank of England and the import licensing branch of the Board of Trade. The Overseas Finance Division was thought of as the primary source of official advice on general policy in the financial field, while the Board of Trade

[1] Lord Morrison, *Government and Parliament* (London, 1956), p. 36.
[2] *ibid.*, pp. 299–300.

was responsible for commercial policy in the narrower sense of the encouragement of exports.[1]

The activity of the Treasury was, however, relatively less important in the period after the principal international organizations had been set up than during their formative years. By 1952, the main impulse towards European economic co-operation had largely been exhausted and the big OEEC operations, the division of dollar aid, the creation of the EPU and the liberalization of inter-European trade, had been completed. There was also, in 1952, a strengthening in Whitehall of the position of those who believed that the original arrangements which had bulked so large in the preceding years were likely to be temporary, and that Britain should look forward to a wider multilateralism on the original Bretton Woods lines.

The organization of the Treasury in this period reflected its decreased activity in the European field. By the end of 1952, the non-departmental chairmanship of the inter-departmental committees no longer required the full-time work of a Treasury third secretary who could now manage it together with the work of the central economic planning staff, which contracted also. Between the middle of 1955 and the end of 1958, the separate identities of these organizations were merged in the Home and Overseas Planning Staff, but the previous system of separate staffs reporting to the same third secretary was then restored.

The position of the Bank of England, which, in the pre-war period, had possessed a considerable degree of autonomy in its overseas dealings, was much affected by the increase in the direct activities of governments. On the other hand, the connections between the Bank of England and other central banks were retained, and this provided it with important sources of information about the general situation of the world economy. As far as the banks' external relations were concerned, the subject has recently been investigated by the Radcliffe Committee on the working of the monetary system, and the relevant paragraphs from its report may be quoted.[2]

'In most cases (international financial) institutions are set up

[1] See the article by R. Marris, 'The Position of Economics and Economists in the Government Machine', *The Economic Journal* (December 1954).
[2] Cmnd. 827 (1959), paragraphs 331, 332, 333.

by inter-governmental agreement, and the UK is formally represented at the highest level by the Chancellor of the Exchequer
or another Minister. The Bank of England, however, works in
close partnership with the Treasury and other departments of
state in dealings with these institutions, not merely helping the
work of preparation for, but actually participating in, the proceedings of the institutions; for instance, the Chancellor of the
Exchequer is the UK's Governor on the IMF and the Treasury
provided the UK's Executive Director; the Alternate Governor
for the United Kingdom is an executive director of the Bank of
England and the Alternate Executive Director is a senior Bank
of England official. The Bank's role in the UK's contribution to
the proceedings of other international organizations, such as the
International Bank of Reconstruction and Development, the
OEEC and the EMA is hardly less important, if not given the
same formal recognition as in the case of the IMF.

The Bank of England is, in its own right as the central bank
of the UK, a member of the Bank for International Settlements
(BIS). Since the war the BIS has been largely concerned with
short-term operations between European central banks. . . . In
addition to these functions of its own, the BIS was appointed as
Agent for the OEEC for the operation of the EPU (and subsequently the EMA) and carries out certain operational functions for other international institutions (including, for instance,
the International Monetary Fund and the ECSC). Apart from
the close connection between the Bank of England and the BIS
in day-to-day operations, the periodic meetings of the Board of
the Directors of the BIS provide opportunities for the Governor
of the Bank of England and his senior colleagues to have regular
and intimate discussions with their opposite numbers in other
European central banks.

This external side of the Bank of England's work is necessarily
bound up with other aspects of the external economic policy of
HMG, and all who are responsible for the day-to-day operations
recognize that there must be close co-ordination with the other
organs of government particularly concerned with external
economic relations. Many of the Bank's operations are, however,
highly technical and must be handled exclusively by men who
are experts in the techniques of operation and management.
Moreover, technical considerations as to what is operationally

feasible or desirable themselves set limits to the decisions of policy, or help to determine the form and direction which policy takes. In this field it is peculiarly difficult to divorce the framing of policy from the carrying out of operations, especially when the latter are in the hands of experts whose technical brilliance is admired the world over. It would therefore be misleading to describe the Bank as undertaking no more than technical operations and the related international negotiations. It is inevitable that the Bank should also be making an important contribution to the formation of policy in this field.'

The Board of Trade was particularly concerned with the liberalization of trade begun by the OEEC in 1949 and thenceforward the influence of the Board and of its second secretary in charge of overseas work was very marked.

To follow the organization of the Board of Trade in respect of its responsibilities with regard to international organizations, it is necessary to go back to the abolition of the separate Department of Overseas Trade in 1946. Its immediate successor was the Export Promotion Department of the Board of Trade. At this time there was also in existence a Commercial Relations and Treaties Department, which was concerned with the formation of external commercial policy. On January 1, 1949, these two departments were merged into the Commercial Relations and Exports Department.

The CRE is thus the part of the Board primarily concerned with overseas matters, but the General Division of the Board is concerned with general economic policy and monetary affairs, and will probably also be represented at meetings of the GATT and OEEC, though relying on the CRE to keep it in touch with day-to-day developments in these organizations. The Tariff Division of the Board is also important as providing the link between the CRE and the sections of the Board that deal directly with particular industries.

In 1959, the CRE itself was fivefold in structure. One of its divisions dealt with commercial relations and preference questions generally, including GATT. The second dealt with the Sterling Area countries, Canada, Japan and the Colombo Plan. The third dealt with the OEEC, the Council of Europe, the Common Market, the European Coal and Steel Community and the Free Trade Area negotiations then in progress. The fourth dealt with the Far East, the Middle East, the 'iron curtain' countries, and consequently the ECE and questions of the export of strategic materials. The fifth dealt with commercial relations with the remaining countries of the world, and with general questions of trade negotiations.

The Board of Trade has been directly concerned with the European Productivity Agency set up by OEEC in 1953.[1] British industry has not made much use of the services offered by the EPA, but the connection has been maintained largely for political reasons. The National Production Advisory Council for Industry, nevertheless, asked that there should be closer consultation with British industry on the work of the EPA and an Advisory Committee was set up to discuss policy with the British representative on the governing body before the meetings of the latter.

The Ministry of Power has had important international activities in connection with the European Coal and Steel Community as has already been seen. It is also represented on inter-departmental committees concerned with the European organizations and with NATO. These inter-departmental committees have set up working parties on specific issues on which the Ministry may need representation and there are, of course, informal contacts between the Ministry and the Treasury, the Foreign Office and the Board of Trade.

In OEEC, the Ministry is represented on the principal committees dealing with fuel and power, although there is little direct interest in these questions except in so far as they affect coal exports, since from the energy point of view Britain is still an island. Nevertheless, it has been desirable to maintain membership of such committees because of the importance attached by Britain to one of them, namely the Oil Committee. The Oil Committee performed an invaluable executive function in dealing with the scarcity of oil at the time of the Suez crisis. It was possible rapidly to gather experts from the principal countries concerned, and since all these had the same basic interest as importers of oil, and since there was accumulated experience from the post-war shortage, the machinery functioned in a highly satisfactory manner.

[1] *European Year Book*, Vol. III, pp. 22–3, p. 205.

The Ministry is also interested in the future problems of energy in Europe into which the atomic energy question enters. These have been dealt with in two bodies; the Energy Committee representing all the OEEC countries and dealing with general problems not covered by the committees on individual fuels, and the Energy Advisory Commission concerned with long range estimates.

The fact that Britain is an island also limits the work in the international field of the Ministry of Transport. The aviation side of its activities (now concern the new Ministry of Aviation) have bulked largest through the International Civil Aviation Organization and its regional bodies, such as the Annual European Civil Aviation Conference. For this purpose the Ministry of Transport has had, in the past, an under-secretary looking after overseas policy generally. Meetings of the ICAO and of the European Conference have been attended by delegations from the Ministry. Their work has been primarily technical but has included some economic aspects. The Ministry of Transport has also, in the past, been responsible in conjunction with the Foreign Office for the negotiation of treaties affecting air traffic and conventions governing the safety or operation of ships or aircraft.

As far as land transport is concerned there have been studies under the auspices of the United Nations, and in 1956, the United Kingdom became a member of the Berne Convention on Railways with the object of trying to simplify the conditions for the passage of goods and passengers to and from the continent. Similar work, designed to standardize the rules of European road transport, has been done by the OEEC, the ECE and other bodies, and the European Conference of Ministers of Transport holds a watching brief over all the European activities in this field. A lot of the work of this body is, in fact, done for it by committees at OEEC. The Ministry of Transport has tried to prevent the ECMT doing work which can be done by other European bodies, but, of course, unless and until a channel tunnel or channel bridge are built, it is understandable that all this work should be regarded as less important by the British Government than by Continental ones. It has been pointed out that 'in connection with land transport the world is suffering from a surfeit of international bodies with active secretariats pursuing studies and producing proposals of little value except to call for larger and more frequent conferences and bigger and more powerful secretariats. These conferences make heavy demands upon officers in various sections of the Department.'[1] Although this is one way of looking at the impact of such organizations upon a basically domestic department of this kind, it has also been pointed out that some of the international studies, for instance on railway finance, the use of road transport for goods, or questions of road safety, have a direct utility since Britain's problems are not unlike those of the continental countries. All this work is handled by a small division in the Ministry called the International Inland Transport Division, headed by an assistant secretary whose entire time is taken up by all this work. A lot of his time is spent abroad and, in addition, specialists are sent to international committees as the need arises. The permanent OEEC delegation in Paris is little involved with the joint working parties between the ECMT and the OEEC. Although the assistant secretary concerned with this work in 1959 had held the position for a number of years, it was not the general intention of the Ministry that people should specialize overmuch in these international aspects of its responsibilities.

Of the other domestic departments the Ministry of Labour is probably the one with the greatest amount of international work.[2] This is primarily due to the fact that responsibility for relations with the International Labour Office was given to the Ministry in 1921, and the Ministry has always held that this position should be maintained, the Foreign Office and other departments being consulted as necessary.

The position of the Ministry of Labour in this respect has been retained despite the fact that the organization itself has shifted its emphasis in the post-war years from the negotiation of international standards of social policy to the development of co-ordination and mutual assistance among nations with a view to achieving a greater general measure of social welfare. More general debates have largely taken the place of the effort

[1] Sir Gilmour Jenkins, *The Ministry of Transport and Civil Aviation* (London: Allen & Unwin, 1959), p. 20.
[2] See Sir Godfrey Ince, *The Ministry of Labour and National Service* (London: Allen & Unwin, 1960), Chap. XII 'International Labour'.

previously spent in elaborating conventions and this has made the national delegations more important as compared with the ILO's own staff. The expansion of regional activities has also complicated the machinery since there are now the problems of technical assistance in Asia, Africa and Latin America.

The machinery of the ILO consists of the general conference, the Governing Body and the International Labour Office controlled by the latter. There are also regional conferences and industrial committees. Thus the impact of the work of the ILO on the Ministry is necessarily uneven, rising to a peak in connection with the annual conference in June and the regular meetings of the Governing Body in November, March and May. Britain is also a member of the European and Asian Regional Conferences and of the new African Conference. Finally there is an African Advisory Committee and three or four Industrial Committees every year, and of these Britain is always a member.

The organization of the Ministry of Labour includes an overseas department which looks after nearly all overseas questions including relations with the ILO. Questions involving labour or social matters, dealt with by other international organizations, are handled by this department, though in these cases communications have to be routed through the Foreign Office. One branch of the Overseas Department deals particularly with OEEC and NATO and the assistant secretary in charge of it is actually the chairman of the OEEC Manpower Committee. The branch dealing with the ILO deals also with the WEU and the Council of Europe. A third branch of the Ministry's Overseas Department deals, among other matters, with the labour attaché services at the embassies. Labour attachés are assigned to ambassadors and considered members of their staffs. With a single exception, however, all of them (in 1959) were seconded from the Ministry. At the Foreign Office itself there is an official detached from the Ministry of Labour who has the rank of assistant secretary and is called the advisor to the Secretary of State on International Labour Matters. He looks after the labour attachés in co-operation with the Overseas Department in the Ministry. Other contacts that have to be maintained are with the Colonial Office owing to the ILO's interest in colonial questions. Colonial territories can be represented at the Annual

Conference by observer delegations. With the emergence of many of these territories into independence the CRO is now increasingly concerned with the ILO, and was for the first time represented in the British delegation to the annual conference in 1959. Territories that become independent have, of course, the right to separate membership. Contacts will also be necessary with particular Ministries in relation to the Industrial Committees of the ILO, on which the Ministry of Labour's own representative is accompanied by someone from the department directly concerned with the particular industry.

Apart from the ILO, 'Officers of the Ministry regularly represent the United Kingdom on the Manpower Committee of OEEC, Working Groups set up for labour questions by the North Atlantic Treaty Organization, the Social Committee established to advise the Committee of Ministers of the Council of Europe, the Western European Union Social Committee and certain of its Sub-Committees and its Joint Committee on the Rehabilitation and Resettlement of the Disabled: from time to time delegates are provided for other Committees'.[1]

Other domestic departments having connections with international organizations work largely in the same way as does the Ministry of Labour in relation to the ILO except where there is a definite political context to a particular question. There is, however, a greater tendency to use Foreign Office channels of communication, because these organizations arose directly out of agreements between Foreign Offices, for instance, the Food and Agriculture Organization and the World Health Organization, the domestic departments only coming in at a later stage when the precise constitutions of the organizations were being drafted. For instance, in regard to the FAO which is located in Rome the Ministry of Agriculture might ask the embassy to convey its views on some matter to the Director-General.

Although UNESCO falls within this group of organizations it is looked after on the British side by the Ministry of Education where UNESCO matters were dealt with by the under-secretary responsible for Welsh affairs. Since the Universities in Britain are not the concern of the Ministry it is understandable that most of the other cultural activities of international organizations are dealt with on Britain's behalf by

[1] Ince, *op. cit.*, p. 158.

the Cultural Relations Department of the Foreign Office, or by the British Council.

Even when we come to the domestic department *par excellence*, the Home Office, we find that it is by no means free from concern with international organizations.[1] Its responsibilities for civil defence give it a direct concern with one aspect of NATO's work. The British Government is represented by the Permanent Under-Secretary at the Home Office on NATO's Senior Civil Emergency Planning Committee; and the Home Office is also represented on its subordinate committees and working groups. The work of the OEEC in promoting freedom of movement for persons within the European countries again touches the Home Office most closely, and it is represented on the relevant OEEC committee and has, of course, also to participate in the bilateral negotiations with individual countries arising from this committee's recommendations. These responsibilities of the Home Office are carried out by detaching officers from their home duties and the Home Office is not represented on the delegations either to the OEEC or to NATO.

This cursory and incomplete review of the impact of the international organizations upon the Whitehall departments shows the extent to which nearly all of them are now directly concerned with fields of activity of an international kind as are the boards of the nationalized industries.[2] It is in many cases, as in the case of the Foreign Office itself, difficult to disentangle precisely the additional burden of work caused by the existence of the organizations themselves from that produced by the general extension of governmental activity into new fields; but the problems created are of the same kind. There is the problem of co-ordination arising from the necessity of seeing that the different departments are conducting their own external relations in line with the general policies of the Government. And there is also the question as to whether the officers of these departments are suitably equipped for the relatively new role of international negotiators which has thus been thrust upon them.

[1] See Sir Frank Newsam, *The Home Office* (London: Allen & Unwin, 1954), Chap. XVI, 'The International Work of the Home Office'.

[2] cf. the table, 'Responsibilities of Departments—other than those exclusively concerned with External Affairs—for relations with International Organizations' (1956) in Chester and Willson, *The Organization of British Central Government*, pp. 205-6.

CHAPTER 7

Problems of Co-ordination

WHEN we come to the methods by which policy is co-ordinated we are faced with conditions which differ from those of the previous part of the present enquiry. While the articulation and internal organization of government departments individually is, with certain obvious exceptions, a subject upon which it is thought possible for the general public to be kept informed, the methods by which the activities of these departments are co-ordinated are matters reserved for official knowledge only. Or, at least, this is the case except in very broad outline. What this amounts to is that no public reference is made to either of the principal methods of co-ordination: that is to say to Cabinet committees at the ministerial level, and interdepartmental committees at the official level, whether or not the latter parallel a ministerial committee in the same field. These inhibitions are basically constitutional. It is held that the collective responsibility of the Cabinet would be infringed if the mechanism through which it arrived at its decisions were revealed, and that the nomenclature and membership of official committees should be kept secret for the same reasons as apply to the other methods by which ministers are advised, and the nature of the advice that they receive. It is, therefore, only possible here to deal with this subject in a very general way.

Reference has been made in an earlier chapter of the present work to the method evolved in the years immediately after the war for maintaining co-ordination between the policies put forward by Britain in a number of international organizations, mainly connected with the United Nations. In this case, however, the work of the organizations in question was very largely of a technical kind, and did not raise for the most part any important questions of policy. It is obviously a very different matter when we come to the major fields of economics, defence and foreign policy, which have been the affair of the international organizations with which this study is more particularly concerned. Here the decisions that have to be made go to the very heart of policy, and the likelihood of important differences of opinion is much greater.

There may be two different, though not altogether separable, sources from which differences of opinion may spring. The general tone of a particular department may be different in some field from that of another department also concerned, and its view on the instructions to be given to British representatives at some international body may consequently have at least a different emphasis. Or the minister at the head of the department may take a different view of what is feasible because of the different political or sectional pressures to which he is submitted. What may, for instance, in a trade negotiation appear an acceptable concession from the point of view of the Chancellor of the Exchequer or the President of the Board of Trade, may look very different to the Minister of Agriculture who may have to defend it to his own particular clientèle.

It is in order to remove such difficulties, through preliminary consultation, that the structure of committees exists. As far as possible the demands of governmental efficiency will mean that efforts will be made to resolve such differences of view before they reach Cabinet level, but this does not mean that the views of the ministers can be ignored at any stage in the process. In as far as the structure of official committees is concerned, it is held that their work is rendered easier, at any rate nowadays, by the general acceptance in Whitehall of the view that their responsibility implies that all civil servants are working for the same ultimate master, and are therefore ready to pool their knowledge and seek for agreed solutions without trying to, as it were, score points off each other. From the point of view of those most satisfied with the system as it stands, it is held that policy itself is now the product of co-operative endeavour, at least between the principal departments, and that it is not of great importance whence the initiative comes, or who the person is who is delegated to present the point of view arrived at. Even those who are more critical admit that the committee system is efficient and does produce agreed positions, which give Britain an advantage compared with countries where the administrative machine is less highly integrated. On the other hand, just because of the variety of interests that British negotiators have to take into account, particularly on the economic side—and here the importance of the Commonwealth aspect of things is obvious—it may be that the positions arrived at are over-rigid and that British negotiators have too little elbow room in consequence.

There is some difference of opinion as to the extent to which the formal work of the interdepartmental committees is the important thing, and how far now, with the well-established close contacts between the departments, this work can be done on a more informal basis, through personal talks and even telephone calls. It looks as though on the economic side the committee structure has retained its importance. For instance, a high official concerned with the Board of Trade's external responsibilities estimated that committee meetings took up about a third of his working time.

One way of preventing this work taking up too much time is to allow a considerable variation in the active membership of a committee as compared with its formal membership; that is to say that a department can choose to be represented by someone on a different level from the officer formally assigned to that committee, if it is a question of a particular topic upon which some other officer has more information, and is better able to represent the department's point of view.

We have pointed out already the importance of the Cabinet Secretariat, and of the Secretary of the Cabinet, in providing the facilities for Cabinet Committees. The services of this Secretariat are accepted by departments, and are of value, because it is regarded as a disinterested organization which can take an objective and impartial view on questions where departmental interests conflict. This reputation for impartiality is strengthened by the manner in which the Secretariat is staffed. Except for a very few of its most senior members, the staff of the Secretariat is drawn entirely from men seconded from other departments for relatively short periods. Continuity is secured by the fact that the Secretary of the Cabinet himself is normally in post for a long period of years—there have in fact been only three since the Secretariat was instituted in 1916. The Deputy Secretary may also remain in post for a number of years. But the remainder of the staff are on short-term secondment—under secretaries staying for only three years and the remainder of the staff for only two. The staff are drawn from the Home Civil Service, the Foreign Service and, to a small extent, from serving officers in the armed forces. The latter were more numerous before the creation of the Ministry of Defence. Thus, the recognition that the Cabinet Secretariat is in no sense an official élite and that its members are migratory birds, who served until recently in ordinary departments and soon will do so again, makes the departments more ready to accept their disinterested services as secretaries of the various committees within the Cabinet Committee structure.

We have already had frequent occasion to discuss the network of committees under Treasury non-departmental chairmanship which has been responsible throughout the period for co-ordinating a policy in relation to OEEC and other international economic bodies. In relation to this group of committees, the role of the Cabinet Office is limited to providing a secretariat. All the rest of the responsibility remains with the Treasury as the sponsoring department. This is natural since when in 1953 the economic section of the Cabinet Office was transferred to the Treasury, the Cabinet Office lost the only section which had a policy making role. It was, therefore, for the main policy making department, in this case the Treasury, to take the lead, and this argument was reinforced by the fact that the Chancellor of the Exchequer was the chairman of the OEEC. Once again, from the point of the Cabinet Office, it is felt that its acceptability as an administrative device is enhanced by its lack of policy making functions.

We have already noted in dealing with the Treasury the fluctuations in the amount of work following upon the machinery of co-ordination which became a regular part of the Whitehall landscape in the period 1952-6. Between 1956 and December 1958, however, there was a new burst of activity because of the negotiations for the proposed Free Trade Area. During this period the main work on the European side was concentrated on this project, although there were a number of special committees within the general structure, each with its non-departmental Treasury chairman and the appropriate membership for dealing with relations with the ECSC, Euratom, the European Nuclear Energy Agency, and such OEEC problems and activities as were not directly connected with the fundamental problem of relations between the new European Economic Community and the other OEEC countries.

The immediate task of the co-ordinating committee has been the drafting of instructions to the British delegate to OEEC or to other negotiators within the field that it covers. When, for instance, the head of the British delegation to OEEC sends a telegram to the Foreign Office, its prefix ensures immediate distribution to about 100 persons. The matters raised in the telegram are taken up by the Mutual Aid Department of the Foreign Office and also by the interdepartmental committee organization in the Treasury. It is for the latter to see that any necessary action is taken in the way of getting interdepartmental agreement to the next step to be taken, while it is the business of the Mutual Aid Department to see that the answer to the telegram is forthcoming.

The small department which works for the chairman of the principal committee enables rapid action to be taken, and the use of telegrams and telephones rather than formal letters and the circulation of drafts, has speeded up action so that telegrams can sometimes be answered within an hour or two of their receipt. Although the work is primarily economic, this machinery enables the Foreign Office's point of view to be taken into account at every stage.

People who have been concerned with operating this machinery have suggested that several conditions must be met if it is to be successful. One of these is that either no department must be regarded as being in the lead, or the department primarily concerned must accept its responsibility. The chairman must not be regarded as committed to the views of a single department, and other members of the committee must be at policy making level and attend as individuals, not allowing themselves to be represented by deputies who might have to refer back for instructions. Finally, it must keep to its task of co-ordination and take care lest it should be tempted to substitute itself for the departments since, in the last resort, the departmental Minister is the person answerable for the policy decision arrived at. It is this sense of the individual responsibility of the departments, as existing alongside the general Cabinet responsibility for policy as a whole, that colours the attitudes towards this system of the entire civil service.

It would be difficult to discuss this work in greater detail without impinging either on the sphere of policy or entering into questions of personalities. A delicate balance obviously needs to be maintained between the delegation or delegations that have to negotiate with their international colleagues and the civil servants at home. It may be desirable that the initiative should come from one source or the other according to circumstances. It is, above all, important that the machinery should not become overloaded so as to create difficulties in producing rapid responses to rapidly changing situations.

On the whole it would appear that in this field there has been agreement that the system that has been worked out suits British needs, both as regards the current subject matter of international economic work, and in respect of Britain's particular institutional structure. To recapitulate, there has for a number of years been a main committee representing the departments primarily concerned, with the Treasury, the Foreign Office and the Board of Trade as the three essential ones. This committee has had a non-departmental and independent Treasury chairman with a small staff of his own, and a secretariat provided by the Cabinet Office. The committee has reported, where appropriate, to the committee of permanent secretaries concerned with economic work under the chairmanship of one of the two joint permanent secretaries to the Treasury, and the collective advice of the officials proceeds further to any appropriate ministerial committee or to the Cabinet itself through the Chancellor of the Exchequer who is now established as the Minister in charge of economic policy as a whole.

The co-ordination of policy in relation to NATO has naturally been affected by the changing emphasis in the work of the organization itself. The 'annual review' which as we have seen came into effect after the Lisbon meeting means that each country has to say annually what its defence effort will look like at the end of the year in question, what can be expected from it the subsequent year, and finally, what in broader terms, are its objectives for the year after that. The memorandum dealing with the country's economic position in relation to these defence requirements is also being considered by the Council.

In order to avoid duplication with the work being done by the OEEC, it was originally agreed that the economic section of this annual review for NATO should come just after the OEEC'S annual economic review. NATO could thus take as given the broad conclusions of the latter about a particular country's economic position, and concentrate on deciding whether its allotment of resources to defence was adequate. This procedure presented each individual country with the temptation of trying to prove that its own defence effort was very great in relation to its economic circumstances, while the other countries were put in the position of trying to prove that its effort could be still greater.

For the British Government it was necessary to co-ordinate the presentation of its position to NATO with its presentation to OEEC. It was therefore desirable that the same group of people should work on the documents to be presented at the two reviews. Use was made of a special sub-committee of the main committee for economic co-ordination. The main committee itself dealt with the principal questions that involved both military and economic considerations. For instance, when the Americans offered machine tools to countries willing to use them for increasing defence production, and actual weapons to countries which could not produce them, Britain had to decide whether it would be harmful to the economy to accept machine tools and turn over to armaments part of the country's resources which might otherwise be producing for export markets.

The change in atmosphere in 1953–4, when it became clear that it was not economically or politically feasible further to increase the level of Western armaments, diminished the importance of the existing machinery for handling the economic side of NATO. The economic section of NATO's annual review was no longer dealt with by a special sub-committee but was now drafted in the Treasury itself, and it was in the Treasury also that the necessary co-ordination was effected with the OEEC annual memorandum.

In 1956 a feeling spread in Great Britain and the other countries of the alliance that even the existing rate of the defence programme was too high. The NATO Council therefore decided to work out a new political directive for the military authorities, in the light of which they were to work out their new military requirements. In order to handle the British side of this work, a special sub-committee of the principal official committee dealing with NATO was set up to brief the negotiators. This special sub-committee included the Permanent Secretary of the Ministry of Defence, a Second Secretary from the Treasury, a deputy Under-Secretary of State from the Foreign Office and the Chief of the Defence Staff. The permanent representative on the NATO Council was also normally invited to attend its meetings.

From 1957, it became the practice of this committee to look over the whole of the British annual review memorandum to NATO, which now includes a general explanation of British defence policy, of the defence programme and of its relationship to the British contribution to the NATO forces. The document also contains a separate and more detailed section dealing with each of the three armed services, and a section on the British economy, with particular reference to the impact upon it of the defence programme. The collection, editing and co-ordination of the material for the entire document is the responsibility of the Ministry of Defence. The military sections of it are submitted to the Chiefs of Staff whose views are then reflected in the revised draft which goes to the committee.

Although the members of this committee, other than the permanent representative, are persons who would normally be meeting frequently anyhow, it is useful to have such a committee because it gives them a secretariat. Although it ranks as a Cabinet committee, its secretariat is provided jointly by the Cabinet Office and the Ministry of Defence. The existence of this small committee has meant that meetings of the principal official committee became unnecessary, although it continued in existence on paper. It will be seen that there is a contrast between the methods used on the defence side of government and those used on the economic side, arising largely out of the fact that the Ministry of Defence is itself a co-ordinating department. For instance, as has been seen, the preparation of the military section of the annual NATO memorandum does not require an elaborate committee organization. Again, the business arising from the British contribution to NATO's infrastructure programme is handled directly by the Ministry on whose vote the expenditure is carried. The Ministry of course calls in people from the service departments and other departments where necessary.

The existence of the Ministry of Defence also simplifies the co-ordination of instructions to the NATO delegation. Anything that comes up in the NATO Council involving the services will come back to London for their comments. The Chiefs of Staff will discuss the matter with a representative of the Foreign Office and take the necessary decision. It will then be passed back from the Ministry of Defence to the Foreign Office for transmission to the delegation. The Foreign Office will not normally have contacts with service departments themselves except on matters of detail. Otherwise it will assume that they have been consulted by the Ministry of Defence. The Permanent Under-Secretary's department in the Foreign Office is responsible for liaison with the Chiefs of Staff organization, and representatives of the Foreign Office sit on a number of interservice committees. One of them is chairman of the Joint Intelligence Committee. If serious differences arose between the Foreign Office and the Chiefs of Staff they would have to be resolved by the Defence Committee of the Cabinet.

The variety of NATO's functions will, however, at all times, call for a flexible instrument of co-ordination in Whitehall. For instance, a fairly late development inside the organization of an interest in scientific research meant the establishment of new contacts for the delegation in that field.

Emphasis has already been laid on the importance of the experience gained by individual officers through their employment directly by NATO. When, for instance, SHAPE wishes to recruit an officer from Britain, the notification comes to the international defence organizations section of the Ministry of Defence. They call upon the relevant service ministry to nominate an officer, but once he is nominated, the Ministry of Defence sees to his appointment. Many of the posts follow an automatic rotation, but the filling of the senior ones would be discussed by the Chiefs of Staff. In this respect, as in other aspects of relations with NATO, no important criticism of the machinery on the British side has been noted.

Formal machinery is not the only way in which co-ordination

of policy is achieved. Those who have to work the machinery must be attuned to each other and find it easy to work together. How far has the recruitment and training of government servants in the period adequately allowed for the new responsibilities of government and the new techniques which they involve? Is there a difference here between the foreign service and the home departments?

There would seem to be general agreement that the Government's new economic responsibilities have called for persons able to handle problems of a new kind. It is believed that those responsible for shaping and controlling the machinery of government have been well aware of this need, and have tried to produce and promote persons most suitable for this type of work—not departing on the whole from the normal tradition of the British Civil Service that people learn best on the job without pre-selection or formal training. Experience is relied upon to differentiate between those who think and express themselves most easily in words, and those who have a numerical or quantitative bent.

Criticism of this empirical approach to the problem has come, in the first place, from those who believe that academically trained economists ought to play a much larger part in modern British Government.[1]

As far as recruitment to the administrative class is concerned, quite a large number now come in with academic qualifications in economics. Between 1948 and 1959, of those admitted as assistant principals, sixty-seven (or about 10 per cent) had read economics, and sixty-one (or about 9 per cent) had read the Oxford School of PPE (philosophy, politics and economics). In addition, there are approximately ninety posts in different departments, for instance, the Colonial Office, the Board of Trade, and the Ministries of Agriculture, and of Housing and Local Government, covering specialized work of an economic character, for which a degree or a post-graduate qualification in economics is required. Over twenty posts of this kind were filled by recruitment from outside between 1957 and 1959.

[1] See R. Marris in the *Economic Journal* (December 1954), p. 783; and for a more extreme exposition of the same viewpoint the article 'The Apotheosis of the Dilettante' by Thomas Balogh in Hugh Thomas (ed.) *The Establishment* (London, 1959).

As far as the economists in the administrative class are concerned, some people feel that there are still too few of them, and that those who do come in are shunted into purely economic work and not used to leaven the thinking of the service as a whole. They also feel that too little formal training in economics is given to persons already in the Civil Service. There is indeed a course on elementary economic concepts attended by some but not many Treasury and other home Civil Service officers. But this is not regarded as sufficient. It can, however, also be claimed that the general demands of administration call for different kinds of ability, and that too many economists would be a distorting factor. Others point out that there is no evidence that a flourishing school of academic economists is an assurance that a country's economy will be well handled, and emphasize the importance of practical experience in knowing what to do, and what are the proper limits of governmental action.

There would appear to be a genuine difference of opinion as between individuals, and even perhaps as between departments, as to the extent to which the 'generalists' responsible for policy can make use of specialist advice without themselves being able fully to assess it from a technical point of view. Such problems are not, of course, limited to the field of economics. The role of scientific advisers in defence matters provides an obvious parallel, although this is less directly related to our central theme.

Finally, there are those who believe the distinction between generalists and specialists to be overdone even in the economic field, and who argue that the speed of change today is liable to render much specialist knowledge out of date very rapidly indeed. The real essentials, they claim, are flexibility and imaginativeness. Something like the Free Trade Area negotiations demanded speculative thought on alternative future patterns of trade, which was quite different from the quantitative type of thinking called for in the handling of the European Recovery Programme.

The Foreign Office attitude to the question of economic expertize has been affected by its long-standing need to have officers capable of handling commercial work, and by its belief that although many members of the foreign service have studied economics at the University and have found the

173

training useful in commercial posts, trained economists do not necessarily make the best commercial officers. The Foreign Office itself gives some training, to officers usually immediately before their appointment to a commercial post in order to give them the necessary background. During the seven weeks allotted to the course, they spend some time in the Board of Trade and visit chambers of commerce, shipping companies, banking organizations, Lloyds and other insurance associations, and other branches of economic life. The knowledge acquired on this course, and the experience acquired in his own post, are supplemented whenever such an officer is on leave by further courses involving visits to more industrial and commercial concerns. The general object is to give commercial officers a picture of how other government departments work and of the activities of the City and of British industry. Finally, once a year, a special series of lectures at the London School of Economics is given to an audience of selected members of the foreign service.

It is recognized that the Board of Trade has an interest in the appointments to senior commercial posts. The President of the Board of Trade may be represented if he so desires when senior commercial appointments are considered by the Senior Promotions Board composed of Ministers and officials in the Foreign Office. But although this right has sometimes been exercised, since there is now machinery for close consultation with the Board of Trade about all matters concerning the commerical services including appointments, the Board has not lately considered it necessary to be represented on the Promotions Board. Its views on such appointments are sought in advance of the meetings of the Promotions Board and represented to it by the deputy under-secretary of state for Administration.

The Foreign Office has in the past come in for considerable criticism for its alleged lack of interest in the wider problems of economics. This criticism was stressed in a series of articles published in the *Manchester Guardian* on October 26 and 28 and November 3, 1955, where the economic training in the foreign service was described as 'grotesquely' inefficient. It was alleged that there was a feeling in the Foreign Office that the economic expert was somehow inferior and likely to be passed over for promotion, partly because officers dealing with international economic problems of great political importance were still often called commercial as though they were simply dealing with the promotion of trade. It is certainly the view of the Foreign Office that such criticism is misplaced, and powerful evidence can be produced to show that nowadays experience in economic work is characteristic of a very high proportion of its senior staff. In October 1959 it was possible to give six fairly telling examples. The then Permanent Under-Secretary of State, previously HM Ambassador in Bonn, had been secretary of the Supply Council in Washington during the war. One of the two Permanent Under-Secretaries of the Treasury had previously been Ambassador in Washington and before that under-secretary in charge of economic affairs in the Foreign Office. The Ambassador in Paris had served as a principal assistant secretary in the Ministry of Economic Warfare. One deputy under-secretary of state for Foreign Affairs who had served as Ambassador in Stockholm and Teheran had been secretary of the Supply Council and later, head of the Economic Relations Department in the Foreign Office. Another who had previously been HM Ambassador at Rangoon had been head of the United Nations Economic and Social Department, and then head of the Mutual Aid Department. Finally, another former head of the Economic Relations Department was serving as Ambassador in Baghdad and had previously served as Ambassador in Cairo.

It is true that more far-reaching schemes for giving economic training to members of the service have been mooted from time to time. Ernest Bevin was interested in promoting a scheme along the lines of that prevailing in Belgium, where foreign service officers are seconded on three separate occasions in the course of their career to a bank or other approved economic concern. Mr Bevin's idea was that British foreign service officers should spend such periods in the Board of Trade or the Ministry of Fuel and Power or in a bank or other business. This scheme was however dropped. Now it is thought that a good deal of expertize can be gained by the circulation of people through posts of different kinds. And an attempt is being made to put more good men through the commercial side early in their careers. There is a regular arrangement by which a first secretary is sent to the Treasury, and other officers may be seconded to the Treasury or Board of Trade, while the idea of eventually sending people right outside the service to gain experience is not wholly excluded from consideration. It is now hoped that it will prove possible to make arrangements for seconding members of the foreign service to business firms for short periods. For some years after the war it was difficult to get in the right amount of training because of the necessity of filling all the vacant positions, and even now the shortage of staff is an impediment to more elaborate training.

A different question is that of the new type of multilateral negotiations which now needs to be handled, not just because of the existence of international organizations, but because governments now wish to come to agreements on matters which previously they did not even discuss. In bilateral negotiations national objectives are pre-determined; the object of negotiation is to reconcile those of one party with those of the other, by compromising, where necessary, on their respective demands. In multilateral negotiations, the national interest cannot be settled in advance, but is worked out co-operatively in a 'seminar' atmosphere, more like that of an interdepartmental committee at home. It raises problems of its own with regard to the proper relations between the negotiators on the spot and the parent department or committee. One of the features of the new type of multilateral negotiation is that one can never be certain what is going to come up next. This makes detailed instructions on tactics impossible. It is, therefore, very important not so much that the people in London should go over for the negotiations (though they may well do so from time to time), but that those who negotiate should have the opportunity of making policy at home. They should return frequently and be given a full opportunity of affecting policy. The use of this technique with regard to developments in NATO in recent years has already been noticed.

It has already been seen that home civil servants from a large number of different departments are likely to be involved in negotiations of this kind at some stage in their careers, but very little general consideration has been given to the problem of equipping them for these new responsibilities. Generally speaking, people are simply launched into international work as occasion arises. What has been done, however, has been to give a number of government servants the opportunity of looking at the running of government departments in other countries.

Work familiarizing officials in one country with the practice of others began as a consequence of Article 3 of the Brussels Treaty. A number of general courses were held for explaining the institutions of other countries to the officials of another. These were held annually between 1949 and 1953. In 1951 a sub-committee of the Cultural Committee of the Brussels Treaty Organization was set up 'to promote closer relations between Government officials and other members of the public service in the five countries . . . and to ensure a better under-standing and reciprocal appreciation of the administrative principles and methods of the Governments concerned'. This produced plans for expanding and making more specific the administrative studies already being pursued and also arranged for the exchange of officials for periods between the different countries. In a meeting in August 1955 by which time the BTO had been expanded into WEU so that Italy and Germany were represented, the committee was renamed the Committee for Administrative Studies and in 1956 it became dependent directly on the WEU Council taking the style of the Public Administration Committee which has since met twice a year. A number of courses on the way in which particular countries handle specific administrative questions have been held under the auspices of the Committee and Britain has opened its courses for junior and senior civil servants to officials from other countries. Between 1953 and 1958, forty-five junior officials from the UK had spent periods of up to three weeks in foreign government departments and thirty-seven senior officials had taken part in visits or courses.[1]

The department most conscious of the problems created by new international responsibilities is the Board of Trade, where it is estimated that some three-quarters of its staff have had some experience of work with international organizations or foreign countries. This has been done fairly systematically. The Board of Trade has had since the beginning of the OEEC two or three of its officials on the delegation. And there have always been one or two persons in Washington working with international organizations for part of the time. There is a considerable difference here as compared with the pre-war

[1] WEU Public Administration Committee, *Survey of Activities and Future Plans* (London, 1958).

situation when such contacts were much less widely spread in the department. The Board of Trade has been criticized for moving people too rapidly from job to job, but this at least ensures that a very large number of people get this broader experience.

The Colonial Office, to take another example, has not tried to train a particular set of people for its international work, but has relied upon knowledge picked up in the ordinary course of things. Representing the British case before the Trusteeship Council and so forth, has become almost part of the general training of the Colonial Service officer.

The view has been strongly urged that it would be useful for many civil servants to spend a year or two on the secretariat of an international organization as part of their training. But this view has not commended itself and it has, for instance, been very difficult to get career civil servants to work in the OEEC Secretariat, though NATO does not seem to have had the same difficulty.

There are real difficulties here because of the unattractive nature of much of the work for international organizations, where the cohesion is weaker and the individual less conscious of a strong organization backing him up. Since there is competition between the organizations and the national governments, it is not surprising that it is difficult to get the right men to go, except in a very exciting period of international work, such as the first years of the European Recovery Programme. This of course applies to private individuals as well as to government servants.

The machinery for recruitment to the international secretariats is that when a British national is required, the Ministry of Labour is informed, and it is its responsibility to put forward people with the necessary technical qualifications. If someone is required from a particular British department direct contact is made with it although the Ministry of Labour comes in to organize the transfer.

Quite apart from the domestic departments, the Foreign Office itself has been criticized for insufficient attention to the demands of the new multilateral diplomacy, and it has been suggested that it might still improve upon its handling of international organizations by a greater willingness to draw upon people from other departments or even from outside government service altogether. The author of the articles in the *Manchester Guardian* already referred to suggested that the breadth of interest required in the modern ambassador might make it desirable to fill some top-level posts with political rather than foreign service appointees. The opportunities for promotion thus removed from the foreign service might be compensated for by giving its members opportunities elsewhere in government employment. The writer went further in wishing to go back upon the changes of 1943 severing the link between the foreign service and the home Civil Service and to have representatives of the central establishment authorities on the Senior Promotion Board in the Foreign Office.

This point of view has not found support in Whitehall where the 1943 changes are generally held to have been a success. Nor does there seem to be any significant support for the still more radical view that the contemporary difficulties of distinguishing foreign from domestic policy mean that there is no longer any need for a separate foreign service at all. For one thing there is the very practical obstacle that large numbers of men highly suitable for government employment may be reluctant to commit themselves (and their families) to spending a large part of their lives abroad. It is true that since the war a contingent obligation to serve abroad has been imposed upon newly recruited government servants.

The rules say that 'members of the home Civil Service may be called upon to serve in any part of the United Kingdom or overseas . . . Service abroad is more likely to be required in some Departments (e.g. the Defence Departments, Board of Trade) than in others. Officers in the Commonwealth Relations Service must expect to spend a substantial part of their service in the United Kingdom Missions abroad. . . In the foreign service, transferability between posts abroad as well as between the Foreign Office and posts overseas is an essential condition of service.'

There was no such provision in the regulations for the general service class in the home Civil Service before the war (though there was for certain departmental classes), and civil servants recruited then have no liability for overseas service. Officers who undertake tours of duty abroad receive a not over-generous expatriation allowance as their only compensation for the personal inconvenience involved; but, generally speaking, no difficulty has been experienced in getting the services of those required.

Quite apart, however, from the practical considerations involved, it is argued that critics of the foreign service ignore the fact that the science or art of getting on with foreigners is something as real as economic expertize and just as valuable in its proper place. Further, it is said, such critics ignore the advantage at the senior levels of diplomacy of having a full acquaintance with the whole world wide organization of the foreign service, and of being able to make use of it with the sureness of touch which only long experience can give.

It is natural that there should, over the period, have been some questioning of the success of the representatives of the foreign service in reporting on the kind of developments in other countries which directly affect the likely attitudes of their representatives in international institutions. Such criticism would have been valid for a number of countries before 1914, and even for some countries in the period before 1939. Now, the foreign service fully recognizes the importance of adequate information on economic and social developments abroad, and the necessity of having a wide range of contacts in order the better to understand them. But it would cost a great deal more money to enlarge the foreign service so as to provide for much larger missions to cover these aspects of its work; and the Foreign Office, in this as in other respects, is limited by the funds allotted to it. One has the feeling that the Foreign Office is, perhaps, over-concerned with problems of establishment in its postings, and that it is, perhaps, over-conscious of the need for economy, though this may be the result of external pressure either from the Treasury or from Parliament itself. Finally, expanding the amount of information secured abroad would not, in itself, be very helpful unless adequate arrangements were made at home for digesting and evaluating the information received.

When all these criticisms have been raised and replied to, it is still possible to assert that the argument has not been lifted above the plane of routine administration. It could be argued that the British Governmental system had served the country well in seeing to it that the new and diminishing role of

Britain in world affairs was accepted with the minimum of dislocation. It had made it possible for the United Kingdom to achieve a favourable balance of payments, which was most remarkable. On the other hand, it was more difficult to maintain that it had been equally productive of positive policies for the future. Ministers are too weighed down with day-to-day responsibilities to have much time for long-range thinking, and the administrators are burdened with the task of keeping the machine itself running smoothly.

Some people have felt that the remedy lies in expanding the top level of administration, that there have been too few people in policy-making positions, and that the same faces have tended to re-appear too often in new roles as a kind of stage army. Others argue that to pursue expansion and to relax pressure would actually diminish the likelihood of new ideas emerging, that experience shows that it is precisely the pressure for results which has been so productive of new thinking. They point to the contrast between the years immediately before 1950 and the less fertile years since then, when pressure upon the government service has been less severe.

It is also argued on the basis of foreign experience—for instance in the USA—and on the basis of wartime experience in Britain itself, that too little use has been made of talent outside the goverment service, and that in particular, there has been too little mobility between the academic world and Whitehall. Some civil servants, believing that their function is primarily an administrative one and not a policy-making one, would undoubtedly welcome more external contributions to the general pool of ideas.

There have been some minor experiments in this direction. A few university teachers have been brought into government departments for a couple of years' service, and the Economic Section of the Treasury has made some use of fairly senior academic economists, sometimes for rather longer periods. A few civil servants have been given study leave in universities by means, for instance, of the Gwilym Gibbon Fellowships at Nuffield College, Oxford. Others have had the opportunity of a year's study in the USA, the Commonwealth and elsewhere on scholarships provided by such bodies as the Commonwealth Fund and the Nuffield Foundation. Informal contacts with industry have been developed and two departments have exchanged staff at middle level with industrial concerns for periods of six to twelve months. Henley Administrative Staff College, to which civil servants are regularly sent, also provides a useful meeting ground for civil servants and promising young men from industry. A useful exchange of ideas has resulted from such contacts—though unlike some other countries (e.g. France) Britain does not favour bringing industrial advisers directly into the negotiating process.

The Foreign Office has, at least until recently, made no comparable use of whatever expertize in foreign affairs may be presumed to exist outside the government service, for instance in the circles reached by the Royal Institute of International Affairs (Chatham House). There now, however, appears to be much better co-operation of an informal kind between the Institute and the Foreign Office Research Department. But there is still a marked contrast with the use made of academic research institutions and individual academic experts by both the State Department and the relevant Congressional Committees. This is the more serious perhaps in that members of the Foreign Service being scattered all over the world have fewer opportunities than their colleagues in the Home Civil Service of exchanging ideas with each other.

Both the Foreign Office and the Ministry of Defence seem now aware of the danger of the virtual confinement of serious and informed thinking on questions of foreign policy, and in particular on the role of Britain in the new world of interdependence to government servants.[1] Such isolation may indeed have considerable advantage in developing a central body of doctrine easily communicable to those whose business is with the execution of policy. But it could also be maintained that it is partly responsible for the obvious and disquieting gap that exists between the policy makers and the general public, the failure to make plain the imperative need for closer association with like-minded countries and the manifold dangers of isolation. How far this is indeed the case can only be seen if we place the whole problem within the context of the general constitutional and political structure of the country.

[1] Governmental circles have not been slow to appreciate the utility of the new Institute for Strategic Studies.

CHAPTER 8

An Assessment of the Record

STUDENTS of the British Constitution have rarely, in the past, considered it necessary to pay much attention to the impact upon it of the foreign commitments of government, nor have they modified their indifference in the light of more recent events.[1] Nevertheless, if we are right in concluding that there has been a fundamental alteration in the nature of Britain's external commitments and a consequent development of new administrative devices to deal with them, we would expect the repercussions of such changes to make themselves felt in every aspect of the country's political system.

We have, in fact, seen that with respect to defence there have come into being unprecedented commitments to collective action, leading in turn to the need to agree with our allies upon foreign policies and strategic doctrines which alone make such defence arrangements meaningful. And that means a close coordination at home between foreign policy and defence policy, including the economic implications of both. We have also seen that the practice of submitting national economic policies to international discussion, combined with the more positive economic role of government itself, has produced an elaborate machinery for concerting policy and action between the departments involved.

What questions do these developments raise with regard to our traditional ways of looking at the making and execution of policy? The classical conception is that enshrined in the phrase 'ministerial responsibility'. By this, in the present context, we mean substantially two things: that the minister makes policy

[1] See, e.g., the lack of attention to these topics in the 2nd Edition of Sir Ivor Jennings' *Parliament*, published in 1957, and the 3rd Edition of his *Cabinet Government*, published in 1959.

and that his civil servants are only advisers and executants, and that the minister will, supported where necessary by the weight of the Cabinet, be able to answer in Parliament for the decisions he has taken. If this is to be a system consonant with the basic principles of democracy, it follows that certain further conditions need to be satisfied. Parliament must be able to make meaningful contributions to the discussion of major questions that have to be decided, and must have at its disposal the information required for the purpose. And active bodies of opinion, whether organized as political parties or in 'interest groups'—material or ideological—must have adequate opportunities for participation in the formation of national policy.

There is no doubt that the traditional responsibility of the minister for policy conforms closely to the preferences of civil servants themselves who are happiest, they say, when working for a minister who clearly knows his own mind and will either initiate policy himself or conduct the business of the department in such a way as to enable him to give firm decisions, for or against, in respect of proposals emanating from the department itself. We have already noted the care taken to avoid prejudging ministerial decisions by allowing too much interdepartmental business to be resolved exclusively at the official level, and to see that the minister's role in defending the departments' policy to his colleagues is not, in any way, diminished.

On the other hand, difficult though it is for the observer outside government to be certain on such matters, one must clearly avoid giving too much credence to externals. There would seem to be at least three respects in which the conventional picture requires re-examination. In the first place, the fact that most important matters in the fields we are dealing with involve more than one department, and more than one minister, must give additional weight to the supreme co-ordinator, the Prime Minister. It would hardly be realistic, for instance, to assume that the successive changes of emphasis in British defence policies and consequently in our relations with NATO, have not been at least as much due to the broad approaches favoured by successive Prime Ministers as to the preferences of the incumbents of the Defence Ministry and their senior advisers, who themselves are nominated by and can be removed by the Prime Minister.

If the point is not pressed further here, it is because the enhanced role of the Prime Minister in the British system, despite the deliberate self-effacement of his own official advisers in the Cabinet Office (as compared with the dramatic expansion of the Executive Office of the President of the United States) is the result of tendencies more far reaching than any that arise from the demands of British participation in international organizations.

In the second place, the fact that, on the whole, the departments are, as has been seen, rather chary of seeking outside sources of information and ideas, while the minister for his part is driven by a demanding routine of work, must enhance the role of senior civil servants as initiators as well as advisers. The conventions that forbid the naming of individual civil servants in writing about the recent past must not mislead the unwary reader into underestimating the role of personality in history, even in Whitehall. It is probable that future historians with access to the records will be able to follow important individual contributions in building up the machinery we have been describing, and the basic stock of ideas upon which it rests.

Finally, the strategic position thus occupied by a number of highly placed civil servants is given added importance by the fact that ministers change departments with such frequency as to make it unlikely that they will be there to see the fruits of any seeds they may plant. This disability from the point of view of long-range thinking is inherent in the Cabinet system and has, no doubt, its compensating advantages. Ninety years ago, the great Lord Salisbury commented upon the ease with which the demands of serious planning in defence matters were allowed to be forgotten.

'The perpetual change, which is the normal condition of Downing Street, assists the process of oblivion. The Minister of War does not long remain the same. There have been seven within the last ten years, giving an average of seventeen months to each. The plans of one man are seldom carried out energetically by his successor. One Minister prefers the Militia, and the Militia bask in a brief sunshine of official favour. The next man prefers the Volunteers, and a totally new direction is given to departmental activity. The third Minister is a great believer in the Reserve, and a brand new set of plans is devised and commenced, to give force to his predilections. The fourth Minister looks upon all forces principally with a view to cut them down; and accordingly the successive reforms of his predecessors are consigned to the impartial pigeon-holes, where the children of so many busy brains sleep side by side.'[1]

Clearly, the only obstacle to the possible effects of such discontinuity must lie in the firmness of departmental convictions as embodied in permanent civil servants.

It is hard to be more precise on this point because of the fact that the main policies with regard to international organizations in our period were, on the whole, shared by the two front benches; 1951 would, therefore, in any case probably have marked no major change in this field. On the other hand, there are probably limits to the differences that ministers can make. One need not go the whole way with Lord Esher when he wrote: 'When it comes to a change of government, believe me it is six of one and half-a-dozen of the other . . . all these people are really ciphers. Remember, not more than a dozen people in England count for anything (a large estimate).'[2] But the warning is always worth keeping in mind. Indeed one might add that what prevents an even more dominating role for the permanent servants of the Crown, aside from their own disinclination for it (except in rare cases) is the fact that the practice of some departments, and notably of the Foreign Office, in moving men rapidly from job to job, prevents them also from becoming too expert in a single branch of the departments affairs. The brief tours of duty at home as well as abroad, which the exigencies of the establishment seem to make mandatory, appear completely natural and self-evidently desirable to all, or almost all officials. There is no view with which the non-official mind finds it harder to sympathize, since non-official observers will probably come from a professional background in which life-long expertize in a particular field is

---

[1] 'Political Lessons of the War', *Quarterly Review*, January 1871. I assume that this is one of the articles referred to as Salisbury's by Lady Gwendolen Cecil in the *Life of Salisbury*, Vol. 2, p. 32.

[2] Letter to Admiral Fisher in A. J. Marder, *Fear God and Dread Naught* (London, 1952), Vol. I, p. 324.

regarded as the indispensable condition of success and prestige.[1]

Much more difficult than the question of relations between ministers and civil servants is that of the effect upon Parliament of the Government's new international commitments. We have already noted that the impact of thinking in international organizations, especially upon those members who have had experience of the quasi-parliamentary assemblies, may well be greater than a casual survey of Parliamentary debates would suggest, and that the existence of active party committees to some extent compensates for the lack of a formal structure of specialist committees in the British Parliament on the United States or continental model. But on subjects of a fairly technical and non-domestic kind such as the development of the international organizations and of British relationships to them, nothing but a confronting of Parliament by ministers (or Opposition leaders) with the issues involved, is likely to produce any helpful expressions of opinion, or any constructive initiative such as Parliament has, from time to time, shown itself capable of producing in internal matters.

One is inclined to think that the lack of interest shown by Parliament in these developments during the period was due to a sense on the part of ministers that Parliament was more likely to slow them down than to assist their progress, in that, particularly on the economic side, members would be more prone to stress special elements of the problem—industrial or agricultural protection, Commonwealth preferences and so on —than to take a broad view as to the desirability or otherwise of the general line of advance. If this view is correct, then the responsibility of successive governments is a heavy one. For if it is, in fact, British policy to make the maximum use of the new opportunities for international action, then it is surely essential that the public should be kept reminded of what is taking place and what the limitations are upon the country's freedom of action under modern conditions. As it is, one feels that there is a very large gap between the views held by ministers, officials and those back benchers who have specialized

[1] See, for example, the letter in *The Times* of April 20, 1960, by Mr D. C. Watt of the London School of Economics on the frequent changes in the headship of the Foreign Office Library and Research Department; and contrast the Foreign Office's practice with the handling of University-sponsored Research Institutes.

in the subject and those of ordinary back benchers and the rest of the country.

For these reasons there is something to be said for the opinion that Parliament itself has got to take the initiative that ministers are unlikely to take for it, and for asking whether in the new circumstances the traditional arguments against a standing committee on foreign affairs are as conclusive as is usually believed. The objections to having such a committee are forcibly put by Lord Hankey:

'But there really are considerable objections to the plan of a formal Standing Parliamentary Committee. It would put an almost unendurable strain on the Ministers and staff of a Department already much overworked, and it would constantly put Ministers in the dilemma of having to choose between giving an incomplete account of events, and taking the risk of giving rather widespread knowledge on vital secrets. It is a terrible dilemma. A Minister must be able to tell the truth if he talks to a body like that, but if he tells the truth he does spread secrets too widely.'[1]

But it is not so much the immediate secrets of current diplomacy that need to be, or ought to be made available to such a committee, as the more general considerations which in the Government's view should control the country's long-term policy. Furthermore, the committee should not confine itself to hearing official views but should, to some extent, follow the pattern of the American committees by obtaining information from outside, whether through the collection of written materials or through private 'hearings'—British preferences are likely to make public 'hearings' a highly improbable development.[2]

Such a committee might, of course, limit itself to considering matters directly arising out of British membership of international organizations (other than the United Nations) which would itself eliminate certain zones of great delicacy. This limitation might also meet the case of those whose main

[1] Lord Hankey, *Diplomacy by Conference* (London: Benn, 1946), pp. 170–1.
[2] For an up-to-date view of the American system see 'The Formulation and Administration of United States Foreign Policy'. A study prepared for the Senate Committee on Foreign Relations by the Brookings Institution, 80th Congress, Second Session, 1960.

opposition to the idea of a committee of this kind is based on the view that an essential convention of the British Constitution is the separation of the roles of Government and Opposition, and who hold that even the risk of irresponsible opposition and of possible grave discontinuities is worth running in order to avoid any substantial departure from so vital a principle.

Given the record of political parties in our period in this particular field, it is hard to see where such a committee would have come up against real difficulties due to insurmountable barriers of ideology. For the attitude of the two main parties was throughout affected more by whether they were in Government or in Opposition at particular junctures than by their fundamental ideological preconceptions. There have, of course, within the parties, been strong differences of view in that the Conservatives have contained an element hostile to European economic integration on Commonwealth or protectionist grounds, while the Labour Party has throughout had pacifist, fellow-traveller and anti-NATO elements. The one controversy on party lines came at the time of the setting up of the European Coal and Steel Community, when a Conservative opposition argued that Britain should have gone into the conference that negotiated the treaty. But as we have seen, this made no difference to British conduct after the change of Government in the following year. Both parties reacted to the later conclusion of the Rome Treaties with support for the idea of some form of association between the countries concerned and the remaining members of OEEC, and only the Liberal Party came out in favour of actual membership of the European Economic Community.

The absence of a committee system means that Parliament does not provide a natural focus for the interest groups that may be concerned with the development of the international organizations. The most important of these, the Trade Union movement, has, in fact, taken very little interest in these developments, and has mainly confined itself to seeing that jurisdiction in labour matters is not transferred to an external authority. Generally speaking, the Trades Union Congress has been prone to accept in this field the views of the political wing of the Labour Movement. It has, for instance, been suggested that had the Labour Government taken up a different line on the setting up of the Coal and Steel Community, the Trade Unions would have gone along with it.

Industry, on the other hand, has been much more closely linked with government, and the Federation of British Industries in particular, through the Council of European Industrial Federations and through its own offices abroad and its contacts with foreign Governments and international organizations, has independent sources of information which it may share with Government. There is, indeed, a good deal of contact between the FBI and the relevant departments on an informal basis, which enables industrial opinion to be sounded before a policy is adopted.

On the other hand, formal consultative machinery such as the President of the Board of Trade's Consultative Committee for Industry and its sub-committee dealing with trade and commercial policy matters is more limited where high level policy questions are involved. The difficulties have been analysed with the authority of experience by Sir Raymond Streat, the former chairman of the Cotton Board:

'I refer now to the biggest issues of all, things like GATT and the European Common Market, the nationalization of steel, monopolies, cartels and price rings, financial and credit policies, and wage policies. In such matters as these consultation prior to action is particularly difficult. There are many reasons why it should be difficult. The details depend so greatly on the issues of principle: if the attempt is made to consult extensively before a decision in principle is taken there is danger of provoking uncertainty, unrest and controversy which might injure trading confidence. On the side of industry it is difficult to assemble well-reasoned and fully documented views about a new policy which has every appearance of being quite an abstract issue. Industry is too busy with active problems to relish spending time on theoretical propositions. Industrialists often feel that only government can command the wide range of information on which policy ought to be founded. Civil servants have the right sort of talent for theoretical exercises but if there is no sign at all of a likelihood that Ministers will decide to act on a given matter, investigations within any department tend to be left at a low level and to lack the elements of reality and urgency. It is therefore quite often the case that vital decisions are taken by a Minister who develops firm personal convictions about a particular policy project: he frequently finds himself driven by parliamentary or political considerations to get out a public statement in rather a short period of time and his departmental staff have to do the best they can in a short time and perhaps under limits of secrecy to investigate some of the consequences or complications of the new policy. The result of all this is that new departures of a major kind are often made with little consultation whereas new departures of a minor and non-controversial type can be the subject of extremely detailed and adequate inquiry and consultation. This is a rather ironical consequence of government by politicians but it is hard to see how to avoid it.'[1]

It could be argued that the existence of a parliamentary committee would permit the discussion of these more far-reaching topics.

When we pass from the possible role of Parliament as an initiator of policy and as a link between Government and the public, and look at its more normal constitutional role as the ultimate controller of Government, we do find a sense of discomfort at the implications for it of the development of the international organizations.

It has, of course, repeatedly been argued that ministerial responsibility to Parliament rules out any form of federal organization in which decisions would be taken by an executive authority not responsible to it. For individual ministers would then be unable to answer for it in their home Parliaments. This problem was discussed at length in relation to the Schuman Plan in the House of Commons debate on June 26 and 27, 1950. Sir Stafford Cripps, in defending the British decision not to participate in the discussions, referred to the fact that the proposals were intended to furnish the first concrete foundations of a European federation. Parliament, he said, had always exercised the greatest caution 'as to agreeing to any removal from its own democratic control of any important elements of our economic power or policy' and he was certain he said 'that such caution would be even greater if removal to an external

[1] *Public Administration*, Vol. 37, p. 5.

supranational body were contemplated'. In other words, he took the view that a scheme of the kind proposed could not work unless there was a full transfer of authority to a federal executive, and since it was taken for granted on both sides of the House that this was out of the question for Britain, it involved the rejection of the whole idea. This British viewpoint helps to explain the alternative ideas in British Government circles about the organization of the European Coal and Steel Industries and the abortive proposals for the institutions of the proposed Free Trade Area.

The same concern for the authority of the House of Commons has governed British attitudes towards the Council of Europe. It is widely felt that its members have no responsibility to anyone but themselves and may do more harm than good either by misleading other countries as to the likelihood of British action in a particular direction, or by providing an added platform for the Opposition which, as we have seen, is likely to be represented at greater strength than the party in power.

The question of the participation of ministers themselves in the debates of the Assembly has also raised questions of a constitutional kind. If ministers are not sent it may be taken as showing Britain's inadequate interest in the Council and hence in the European idea; if they are sent they cannot shed their ministerial capacity and have to be guarded as to what they can say. A former Labour Party member of the British Delegation to Strasbourg, Mr George Brown, said in the House of Commons on February 21, 1955, that he was sure that it was a bad thing for a minister to go to Strasbourg: 'A minister there becomes the subject of very great pressures. He gets into great difficulty, and begins sending telegrams back home seeking instructions, just as though he were leading a delegation at one of the executive, Government-backed organizations. He begins to make compromises, just as he would in other places . . . without realizing that when he makes a compromise, although he does so upon the instructions and with the prior agreement of the Government at home—to whom he has sent and from whom he has received telegrams—the people with whom he is dealing are in no position to do the same, because they are members of opposition parties and are irresponsible.'

There is, however, an equal or greater problem when we come

to what Mr Brown calls 'the executive, government-backed organizations', for here there is a genuine dilemma before ministers. If they announce their policy to Parliament beforehand, then they will be unable to participate fully in the give-and-take upon which these organizations depend. If they do not, they may be accused of entering into commitments behind the back of Parliament from which it is now too late to withdraw. On March 26, 1958, the Government refused to give an assurance in the House of Commons as to the view it would take when the Council of WEU discussed a proposed amendment to the Brussels Treaty relating to restrictions upon German rearmament. Mr Aneurin Bevan commented as follows on the Government's reply: 'In various situations with which we are faced we are told over and over again by members of the Government that they will not give undertakings about the policy they will follow in international organizations. After decisions have been made we are told "of course the decision has been made" and we can do nothing at all. It appears that this House has no influence at all upon the decisions of the Government.'

It is understandable, therefore, that it is customary for British representatives, for instance, on the NATO Council, to remind their colleagues that the matters under discussion must ultimately be reserved for parliamentary decision, and although it is possible to use this kind of argument as an excuse for not doing something which the Government does not want to do anyhow, the touchiness in Parliament has to be respected. This touchiness is even more strongly marked when it is a question of pronouncements by officials rather than ministers. On June 7, 1950, at a Press Conference in Paris at which the forthcoming conference about the proposed Coal and Steel Community was announced, the British Minister in Paris said that Britain still hoped that whatever arrangements resulted from the conference some form of association would be worked out that would permit the British Government to join in. In the House of Commons on June 13th Mr Harold Davies said: 'May I ask . . . how it was that Mr William Hayter was able to say that 90 per cent of the people of Britain approved this plan before ever this House had an opportunity of discussing it.'

Finally, there is a considerable degree of sensitivity about the expression by members of the NATO Military Establishment of their strategic views. For instance, when Field-Marshal Montgomery, in May and October 1954, made speeches about the need for NATO forces to use nuclear weapons against an agressor even if the agressor had not used them first, this raised a number of questions in the House of Commons about the political responsibility for pronouncements of this kind.

There is, of course, great force in the argument that if what we attach most importance to, is the responsibility of governments to Parliament and through them to the electorate, then no international organization that does more than facilitate intergovernmental discussion and agreement is fully compatible with our innate constitutional beliefs. It is indeed the logical conclusions of this line of thought that have brought so many Europeans to the point of being willing to accept the idea of supranational executive bodies exercising authority in particular fields and responsible to international assemblies, themselves directly answerable to a European electorate. British opinion has overwhelmingly so far gone the other way. At no time has serious consideration been given to the possibility of accepting executive authorities not responsible to the House of Commons, either directly or indirectly. And many would still argue that much of the expression of devotion to these ideas elsewhere can be dismissed as mere lip-service.

The British, it is said, have strong objections to saying that they will go further than they mean to go in fact, partly for reasons of national temperament—an impatience of oratorical gestures—and partly because a minister may be held to his words in the House of Commons, which is likely to be more alert on such a point than many continental legislatures. But there may be occasions when gestures are desirable in order to create the correct atmosphere for discussion and that British insistence upon the letter of the law, in words though not in action, gives a misleading impression. The British attitude to the movement of labour in Europe, which is more liberal than is generally thought, has been instanced as an example.

But the real British repugnance to supranational machinery in the economic field cannot be set aside. It springs in part from the high degree of internal social integration that the country has achieved, and from the general confidence that its citizens place in its internal governmental machinery. Britain would thus exemplify the view frequently expressed by Mr Gunnar Myrdal, for instance in his book *An International Economy*, that the more successful the nation-state is in handling its affairs, and the greater the degree to which it succeeds in attracting the allegiance and expectations of its citizens, the greater the obstacles it presents to full economic and social integration on an international basis. The British have, on occasion, felt with regard to some supranational proposals that it was not so much that the policies of the proposed institutions would be detrimental to British interests, as that the machinery would be clumsy and inefficient as compared with our own. It may have been an exaggeration of this attitude which led first to a fairly widespread belief that the Coal and Steel Community would break down, and then to scepticism about the probable effectiveness of the Common Market arrangements.

The British have also opposed, though with less intransigence, the other main aspect of supranational organization, the acceptance of majority voting. (As we have seen, Britain was prepared to allow for majority voting to play some part in the International Monetary Fund and in WEU and would have been prepared to do so in the proposed Free Trade Area.) Here, the main question is one of substance. Certain subjects are felt to be so important that in the interests of national security or solvency, the final right of decision must be retained. But it is also partly a constitutional question. A British Government outvoted on an issue involving action would be obliged to defend before Parliament something which it, in fact, regarded as pernicious.

To some extent, of course, this is inevitable in all external relations. Bargains, even of a bilateral kind, involve concessions on both sides, and a government defending a treaty has got to show that what has been given up is justified by the advantages that have been secured in return. Indeed, one of the main advantages urged for multilateral negotiations and for organizations designed to facilitate them, such as the OEEC, is that they enable bargains to be struck on a wider basis, by bringing more items into the final account.

A third point to which protagonists of supranationalism also attach importance, the setting up of precise targets with dates attached, as in the tariff provisions of the Treaty of Rome, in contrast with general undertakings to negotiate, would also appear unattractive to British thinking, which has been very conscious of the rapid changes in the economic climate over recent years and the desirability of retaining the maximum degree of flexibility.

British preference and British administrative traditions have not only helped to determine which organizations Britain should join, but have had their share in the shaping of those organizations in which Britain itself has been an important partner. The British have, on the whole, wished the secretariats of the international organizations to act in the manner of the Cabinet Secretariat at home, that is, principally as a means for facilitating discussions and agreements between the national delegations. They have not expected or desired the secretariats to be important sources of initiative in policy. In so far as this attitude has prevailed it has, of course, been something of a handicap upon the work of the organizations in that the more their scope is limited, the harder it is for them to recruit the best men to their service.

The two major organizations we are concerned with have had rather different histories in this respect. In the early years of OEEC it had a vigorous Secretary-General with distinguished and active deputies, who made the organization itself an important element in the thinking of the time. In more recent years the secretariat has been content to act largely as a sounding-board for the more important delegations.

As we have seen, the contrary has been true of NATO. Under Lord Ismay the machinery was deliberately restricted in its capacity for taking the initiative, while under M. Spaak there have been major developments in a contrary direction. Britain has, of course, accepted the fact that on the military side leadership must, to a very large extent, be a matter for the supreme commanders although no public formula has been found for the political control of their decisions in times of emergency. Nor, of course, with the United States and British deterrents in the hands of the national governments, can it be said that the integration of Western defence has gone as far as the logic of interdependence would suggest that it should. On the economic side it looks as though there may be a partial adaptation to the needs of a remodelled OEEC of some of the forms of organization that have successfully proved themselves in NATO.

The 'Group of Four', which reported to OEEC in April 1960 on desirable modifications in its structure, suggested that in future the Secretary-General should preside over the Council at official level and over the Executive Committee, though arguing that it would be appropriate for a minister to remain Chairman of the Council at ministerial level.[1] This, of course, would differ from the NATO precedent, since under present arrangements the Secretary-General takes the chair at NATO Council meetings at all levels except on purely ceremonial occasions.

The same report, however, also attached the utmost importance to the work of the OEEC in bringing together 'high officials with important responsibilities in the formation of economic policies in their countries', such as the Economic Policy Committee set up in 1959, and suggested that its work might be aided by giving it another sub-committee of restricted membership, which might prove 'useful in ensuring the frequency, continuity and informality of consultations which are essential conditions for the achievement of affective co-ordination.'

It is therefore clear that a strengthening of the position of the permanent staff of the organization would not fundamentally affect its methods of work or the requirements that it makes on individual governmental systems. The merits of the British system are, as we have seen, the care taken to see that the positions of the various departments are co-ordinated prior to negotiation, and its capacity for successful orchestration. Its defects are the converse of its merits—the difficulty of handling a new factor in negotiations if it calls for a decision at ministerial level, and particularly if it involves calling into question a ministerial decision already promulgated. Nevertheless, despite the dangers of over-elaboration, within the framework of inter-governmental activity the merits of the British system would appear greatly to outweigh its defects.

We have also seen that the success of Britain in devising machinery for making the best use of international organiza-

[1] *A Remodelled Economic Organization* (Paris OEEC, April 1960), p. 47.

tions of an inter-governmental kind creates a predisposition to favour them. And, indeed, such organizations have many and genuine merits, even on occasions when they are only a cover for what are essentially bilateral transactions. The main advantage is that the system keeps those who are making the decisions in close touch with the changing positions and attitudes at home. It is of the essence of such institutions that there should be direct and constant contact between their headquarters and the home governments. Provided that the governments themselves have real problems which they think they can best solve through the use of such organizations, they are likely to flourish. But in the absence of such a drive from the governments they rapidly cease to be meaningful.

One must always remember that the organization itself in a case like that of the OEEC cannot say anything publicly about a national policy to which the delegation from the country concerned is not willing to give its assent. This makes the organization, in part, a weapon in the hands of governments for use in influencing their own public opinion. It is, however, true that unless both the secretariat and the delegations which will themselves often tend to become internationally minded as a result of their experiences, are kept very weak, there are always opportunities for points of view to develop which were not necessarily in the minds of the governments when they initiated the organization. In other words, the staff of the organization, with its sympathizers on the delegations, may begin to function as a pressure group, trying to secure backing for its own views in the different countries. And the cynical will add that such views may be conditioned by the natural desire of the staff for the perpetuation of the organization itself.

Such propagandist activity causes undoubted resentment in some quarters, since the international organizations are paid for out of national taxation and since it can therefore be argued that tax-payers in the various countries are inadvertently subsidizing pressure groups. It can also be argued that national policy may be affected by the fact that some pressure groups of this kind are better organized or more vocal than others. It has been suggested that in the British case this may lead to a neglect of general Commonwealth interests since the CRO cannot act in the same way as the European organizations. Whether the record bears out the view that Britain sacrificed Commonwealth to European interests in the period 1947–59 is quite a different question.

Some people regard the creation and expression of points of view independent of the several governments as highly desirable, and applaud the international organizations for precisely those reasons for which their critics condemn them. Other people—perhaps the majority—will base their views on the nature of the policies they themselves prefer, and give their support to those international organizations which have helped to overcome those departmental resistances at home which they personally find most obscurantist.

Another result of the successful handling of the problems set by the international organizations has been, as we have seen, the strong scepticism in Britain as to the possibility of tighter forms of integration. Opinion in Britain has tended to discount the possibility that other countries can surmount the obvious difficulties of supranationalism in a world in which nationalism itself is still so powerful. British opinion has probably under-estimated the strength which the acceptance of mandatory provisions in international treaties has given to governments determined to overcome the vested interests opposed to economic integration, and the extent to which the atmosphere of economic life may be altered by such treaties. It looks, for instance, as though the expectations created among European (and American) industrialists that there would be a Common Market in eight or ten years' time has been more important in determining their investment and marketing policies than the reductions in duties themselves. It has also been discovered that it is possible for such organizations to appeal to particular interests as the best means of securing their own objectives, as seen for instance in the support given by the European trade unionists to the High Authority of the ECSC in the coal crisis of 1958–9. Furthermore, the supranational bodies have shown an institutional flexibility which was, on the whole, unexpected in Britain, particularly as it has partly depended upon judicial interpretation of the basic documents, a method of consti-tutional development hitherto unfamiliar in international organizations.

Some people in Britain have held that had the British been willing to take part in the creation of the supranational organization it would have been possible for her to have secured institutional arrangements more acceptable than those worked out by the Six when left to themselves, and that the sacrifices entailed in entertaining such organizations would have been less than those involved in Britain's exclusion.[1] Continental critics have gone much further and have claimed that Britain's purpose has been not merely to keep out of supranational bodies but to prevent them coming into existence or surviving afterwards.[2] The recriminations which accompanied the abortive negotiations for the proposed Free Trade Area are not intelligible unless this kind of thinking is kept in mind.

Whatever one's views may be on the validity of such continental arguments, it is obvious that the main reason for the advances towards integration made by the Europe of the Six in the 1950s were political. In other words, experience would seem to confirm the prescient statement of a well-known British economist in 1950, when he wrote that 'while economic co-operation may help to pave the way for political co-operation, it has become clear that a strong desire for political co-operation is indispensable for economic co-operation, which can make little real progress without a readiness to sacrifice national interests'.[3] Ten year later the difference in the intensity of the political feeling in favour of closer integration as between Britain on the one hand and the countries of the Six on the other, is much harder to question than it was when these words were written.

It would not be unreasonable to conclude our study at this point. If anything is to be added it must take the form of a more personal and speculative postscript. My own feeling is that it is impossible to assess the record of Britain or of any other country in relation to international organizations in recent years without feeling and there is a clear disharmony between the governmental and administrative institutions available to modern societies and the world in which they have their being. And

---

[1] This is argued with reference to the ECSC, the EDC and the Rome treaties by Anthony Nutting in his *Europe Will Not Wait* (London, 1960).

[2] See e.g. François Fontaine, *Naissance d'un esprit Européen* (Paris, 1958), p. 19.

[3] Sir Donald MacDougall in *London and Cambridge Economic Service Bulletin*, Vol. XXVIII (August 1950), p. 70.

this would be even more obvious if we were to take into account some of the functions of those wider international organizations which we have omitted from consideration.

While it is true that British politicians and civil servants have taken the sovereignty of the United Kingdom for granted, and have deliberately eschewed policies that might have called it into question, it looks as though the picture of a world divided into self-contained autonomous political entities ideally composed of individual nations, has been drifting further and further away from reality. The activities of the individual citizen and the degree of freedom available to his rulers are both increasingly dependent upon forces and institutions that transcend national frontiers. The contrast between the physical facilities available for the speedy movements of goods and people as compared with the political and administrative impediments put in their way, becomes increasingly obvious and less and less generally acceptable. The time taken up in fulfilling the requirements of passport and custom authorities concerned with a traveller by air between London and Paris is longer than that of the actual flight. And it is the flight-time that is likely to be much further reduced in the near future.

Translated into military terms, when to the speed of movement is added the destructive capacity of modern weapons, the impact of these technical changes has been inescapable. Military thought is probably ahead of civilian thought in its readiness to accept the obsolescence of full national independence, since if countries cannot fight independently, the main historic bastion of sovereignty has already fallen. In the last analysis, external sovereignty is the right and capacity to make war.

In economic life the realities of interdependence are prevented from making an equal dent in traditional attitudes by what has already been touched upon, namely the growth of the Welfare State and the increased expectations that it has evoked in its citizens. It would take a veritable revolution in the outlook of the average British citizen to get him to accept the view that decisions at Westminster or in Whitehall are only marginal to his prosperity and progress. Nor can Westminster or Whitehall safely act upon assumptions not held by the mass of the electorate.

We thus arrive at the curious and indeed paradoxical conclusion that the demands which have hitherto been the main divisive factors in international society, namely the demands of war, now exert powerful and increasing pressure in favour of a pooling of sovereignty between like-minded countries, while economic life, once thought of as essentially indifferent to national boundaries, now seeks expression for its needs largely through the machinery of the individual States. How this paradox will resolve itself and what British Government will look like when it does, are matters about which the student of public administration will be wise to avoid prophecy.

Index